The Picture Buyer's Handbook

The Picture Buyer's Handbook

Peter Ford & John Fisher

HARRAP

London

First published in Great Britain 1988
by HARRAP Ltd
19-23 Ludgate Hill, London EC4M 7PD

ISBN 0 245 54236 1

Designed by Gwyn Lewis

Phototypeset by Falcon Graphic Art Ltd
Wallington, Surrey

Printed and bound in Great Britain by
The Bath Press, Bath

Contents

Acknowledgements

We would like to record our thanks to John Gazeley for his initial encouragement with the idea of the book and for his later help over some sections of the text and assembling illustrations. We are also especially grateful to Chloë Jowett, who read the text and made valuable critical comments that had an influence on the final draft. Mr D.H. Farthing of Hadleigh provided the notes and information on which the section on insurance is based, and Susanna Slater of the Eastern Arts Association kindly put together a list of contacts in the other regional arts associations, whose responses to our inquiries have been invaluable in checking details of the list of art collections and galleries in Appendix II. Finally, we would like to thank Pamela Ruff of Harrap for her editorial supportiveness in seeing all the material through its final stages.

The publishers are grateful to the following for allowing them to reproduce material in this book:

Text:
Faber & Faber: passages from **The Artist's Handbook of Material and Techniques** by Ralph Mayer, reproduced on pp.125, 148; Hamish Hamilton: passage from **Diary of An Art Dealer** by René Gimpel, reproduced on p.105.

Illustrations:
British Museum, pp.73, 74, 85; J W Gazeley: pp.52 (lower picture), 57, 93, 95, 113, 114, 115, 116, 117, 118, 119, 121, 132 (above, right); Lacy Scott's, Bury St Edmunds, p.138; National Academy, London: p.67; Press Association: p.144; Royal Academy, London: p.83; Santa Maria delle Grazie, Milan: p.107 (slide from Courtauld Institute); Sotheby's, Bond Street: pp.27, 52 (top picture), 53, 54, 55 (top picture), 56, 57 (top picture), 58, 135, 138 (top picture); Tate Gallery, London: p.80; The Times (photo Tim Bishop): p.21; Victoria and Albert Museum: p.55 (lower illus.), 71, 78, 96, 98; Wilkins & Wilkins: pp.120, 121 (top), 132 (above, left)

The drawing on p.43 is by Carole Vincer. The cover photograph and the one on p.138 (lower illus.) are by Robin Anderson.

It may be that you have a million or so pounds to spare and are thinking of investing in a Rembrandt or, as an alternative, in a wallful of Picassos. If that is the case, then this book has not been written with you in mind. The reader and user of *The Picture Buyer's Handbook* is seen as someone of quite modest means, who may have a bit of money in hand and who is on the look-out for an occupation or hobby that holds out at least the chance of a touch of adventure along with a dash of culture. In other words, he or she will be looking for a diversion from the monotony of jobs and prospects (not to mention the tendency towards a lack of them) in the world we live in today.

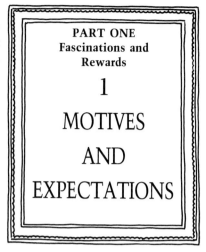

PART ONE
Fascinations and Rewards

1

MOTIVES

AND

EXPECTATIONS

It is a mistake to think that buying, collecting and selling works of art of appeal and merit necessarily means that vast capital sums of money need to be expended. This is an occupation that can be carried out both profitably and pleasurably and kept to a modest scale, provided certain guide-lines remain firmly in view. It is therefore our intention to provide a basic, practicable background to indicate how you can pick up the essential information. This will then help you to lay the foundation on which to build a measure of experience in the field in both personal and practical terms.

THE MODEST
OPTION

There are many other books available to cover the various more specific aspects of collecting and the care of pictures. These tend to be partial in character, or else to be highly specialist. The present book — planned as a survey to cover its field in a broad sense while, at the same time, it avoids getting caught up in too much detail — has been written with the layman and amateur or occasional collector in mind. If you know only a little or nothing about art, then wide reading in the field is to be recommended so that you can build up a stock of useful knowledge. The art market is a phenomenon where you literally never know what is going to turn up next. Unless you are intending to concentrate your energies on one narrow area of specialization, then an eclectic rag-bag of information is the most useful asset you can acquire for yourself.

What sort of pictures should the beginner be watching out for in the auctioneers' sales catalogues? How should the uninitiated approach the mysterious processes of buying at auctions, quite aside from the various outlets that exist for selling and dealing in pictures? What range of basic information do you need to arm yourself with concerning the different techniques used by artists down the centuries to the present day to create their paintings and drawings? In what ways may these same works of art be affected by the passing of time or damaged by unforeseen and accidental hazards? What precautions can and should be taken for their care and conservation; and when it comes to repair or restoration, is it wise to attempt to carry out any of this yourself or should you invariably call in the trained restorer? Answers to all of these questions will be suggested in the pages that follow.

As a prospective buyer, a point you need to realize from the start is that, when it comes to buying, you are going to have to have confidence in your own judgement. Just as you need to develop a 'nose' for something good, so you also need to develop a 'nose' for something doubtful. And, so far as this aspect goes, it is essential for your instincts to be backed by a knowledgeable mustering of facts. In contrast to your own preferences, you will moreover need to be shrewdly aware of the sort of work that other people regard as good or desirable, especially if you are going to take up the idea of selling for profit with any seriousness.

It is essential, too, to pick up more than an inkling of those shifts in changing taste for which the art world is notorious. As has been witnessed and commented on time and time again, one generation's discardable horrors almost invariably exert their charm on the sensibilities of the next. As a result, they come to be both highly prized and eagerly collected — a phenomenon that helps to fuel the apparent ability of the trade to continue renewing itself indefinitely as dealers watch eagerly for the chance to encourage new markets. Yet such precognition is not a knack that can be learned by any one rule of thumb. It is a feeling that can only be garnered by experiencing the current changes and switches in climate even as these are in progress.

So far as you, the readers of the present book are concerned, the motives you may have for making forays into the world of sale-room or country-house auctions are likely to be as widely varied as the possibilities awaiting you. Perhaps it is that you are in search of an alternative source of income, or even of an entirely fresh source. Perhaps you have a notion that you would like to start to build a collection of works by an artist or group of artists for whom you feel a special admiration and interest, and that using the proceeds from buying and selling other work might be one way of financing such an objective. Equally, it may be that the thought of getting yourself tangled up with the problems of profit margins does not appeal to you at all, but you would be perfectly happy to indulge in a flutter here and there and back a hunch as it strikes you. If this is the case, then you will at least have the satisfaction of knowing that it is not quite the same situation that you run into every time you back a horse or a greyhound. When it comes to pictures, then every starter on which you place a wager should finish with a place.

Whatever your intentions towards the art world, and however honourable or dishonourable these may happen to be, then, so long as you keep to the advice given in these pages, you can do no other than add to your life a quota of enrichment. Whether or not you end up a millionaire — and we have to say that, in our view, the prospect is most unlikely — you will, by the time you are through with the operation of picture buying, be better off than when you set out. And when we use the phrase 'better off', we certainly do not intend this to be understood purely in monetary terms. Enrichment will follow as much as anything from the fuller life that results from travelling about, meeting new faces and personalities, gaining aesthetic appreciation and accumulating an awareness of artistic tastes and technicalities in the context both of history and the present time. Along with testing your personal instincts and responses towards pictures, you will have all these gains on the credit side even if you never manage to do more than cover your expenses.

Perhaps the best factor of all on the financial side is the fact that levels of profitability can always be managed entirely within the limits of your preference and discretion. These will, in other words, relate directly to whatever time and energy you wish to devote to buying and selling in the art market. The choice of an objective is yours and nobody else's. On the one hand, you may simply enhance your lifestyle; on the other, you could find you transform it entirely. It is perfectly possible for the investment of time, effort and money to be both flexible and tailored to match whatever developments may come to pass in the pattern of your aims and ambitions.

ART AND COMMERCE

The route that links the artist who creates a picture with the person who becomes its eventual owner may well be complex and varied. It is also true to say, however, that it can be very direct. When the process is at its most straightforward, the owner may step into the role of patron and make his purchase from the artist concerned, having taken his pick from among the array of canvases, drawings or other work in progress which are, in the natural course of events, among the furnishings of any active studio.

The route to ownership becomes somewhat less direct when a picture is, as it may be, acquired from an exhibition in a gallery. The gallery concerned may represent the painter and be, so to speak, his agent. Alternatively, the gallery in question may be one that forms part of the function of a regional or town arts centre. In this case, such a gallery will most probably exist on a grant-aided basis. It will, in other words, enjoy the backing and support of one of the regional or national arts associations who are concerned with placing original works of art before the public and so with fostering the appreciation they are felt to deserve.

It does not follow, however, that a picture bought in a publicly funded gallery or arts centre is necessarily being offered at a bargain price. Living professional artists must continue to exist and hope to gain a margin of financial freedom to enable them to continue working. Grant-aid support for galleries is intended to help artists to do precisely this by providing outlets for their work. Pictures on sale in such locations will be priced at whatever is felt to be their current market value. Meanwhile, the question of which of the present-day works are those you should buy if you wish to be sure of making an investment that will mature in the future is a thorny one indeed.

Considering the whole variety of motives that can come into play in the purchase of a work of art, it seems fair to say that these will, on the whole, involve matters of personal taste and preference. It could be that a certain painting has exerted a special appeal and sparked off something in the mind of its potential buyer. The picture may, for example, depict a local scene that has a special or sentimental association; or it may catch the fall of light or the lie and character of a landscape in a way that strikes a familiar chord quite apart from its being accurately observed.

On the other hand, according to the viewer's predilections, the picture making its appeal may consist of a fantasy or dream image, removed from but taking and transforming the elements of everyday life and using them to express the processes through which the artist's imagination makes its journeys. Or a picture may claim to be no more than an abstract or decorative image, assembled out of shapes and colours that have a harmonizing or stimulating effect; or else it contains the strength to create focal points for business or domestic architectural settings. A limitless range of possibilities exists between active movement and contemplative stillness to present the eye with appropriate and valid symbols by which to interpret the world and the society in which we happen to be living out our days.

We could easily make an extensive list of all the actual and potential reasons for buying a picture. Among them we might include being personally acquainted with the artist, for it is a natural thing to take an interest in and feel affinity for the creative efforts of people we know and like or just happen to have met. Another compelling motive may come about through having been told, by one of those who know, that such and such an artist is on the road to making a name for himself, hence that he deserves watching; it therefore following that a modest investment in the works of the earlier stages of his career is likely to pay future dividends.

Nevertheless, when it comes to putting the whole business of bringing about a union between a picture and its owner into its most basic perspective, we can only say that the work simply struck an echo of delight and prompted the decision. The purchaser obviously felt confident that here he had an object with which he could live, and continue to live, without running into any sense of disappointment.

Whatever emerges from attempts to analyse the reasons for becoming the first-time owner of a painting by a living artist, however, the buyer may, in every circumstance, allow him or herself to bask in the warm luxury of feeling that it has been possible to act as a patron to the arts. A contribution has thus been made to the artist's next crust or two. A positive and praiseworthy step has been taken to help by making sure that a market exists for the work of the artist concerned. The purchaser has, moreover, acquired an original artefact with which to decorate his home, create a point of interest and demonstrate to the world how laudably advanced or solidly traditional his personal style and taste may happen to be.

In the midst of all these causes for congratulation, it could therefore seem to be introducing a discordant note if we draw attention to the fact that many such buyers and patrons are also likely to be carrying, at the backs of their minds, the hope that their investments will pay off in the long run. In other words, that the value of an investment will be maintained and will show a profit in relation to whatever shifts in the value of money itself may occur over the years. There is a tone of calculation and detachment entering into the reckoning at this point that does sound decidedly less warm-blooded than the other incentives we have just outlined.

The relationship between art and commerce is, in the nature of things, always bound to have its uneasy aspects. What an ideal world we should be living in indeed if the only rewards we pursued could be entirely free from the taint of finance. The collector of pictures knows that the return he receives from his ownership hinges on many factors, and that those of individual quality, style and skill stand high among them. He knows that such attributes are not lightly won, and that they deserve to be prized and paid for. He knows that a 'good' piece of work must, in the long term, always represent better value than a 'poor' one, in terms both of satisfying the appetites of the imagination and of justifying the price originally paid for it. The twin intertwining strands of value and quality are not, in practice, at all easy to separate from one another.

The art that is being created in the present must inevitably be fraught with difficulties of judgement for the collector. Time, as has been correctly said, is the leading arbiter in questions of taste and fashion. No one, whatever expertise they may lay a claim to, can safely take it on their shoulders to predict what works or types of work the world will be clamouring to get its hands on fifty years from now. The prices being fetched in the 1980s by the paintings of certain living or recently dead artists may well, by the twenty-first century, have an absurdly inflated look to them. On the other hand, the work of certain of their contemporaries may seem as though it was seriously undervalued, if not entirely passed over, by the *cognoscenti* of our own time. In particular, we may expect to find many a reputation taking a bad fall in the American arena of arts sales, where there is an especially insistent emphasis on what is thought to be rising, new, successful and assertive. The counterweight to reputations that rise like comets must surely be that many of them will end in eclipse and outer darkness.

Once, however, we have acknowledged the truism that the art that survives is art that has stood the test of time, it may well be valid to ask which test and which time do we have in mind? An artist whose name has been scorned for a century or more may, without any warning, start to go through the process of dramatic rediscovery. Why it should be happening, no one can say, but all at once the prices being obtained for his works are breaking sale-room record after record. It has become, almost overnight, a worthwhile enterprise to ransack attics and seek out, from where they have been languishing through many decades, any canvases, drawings and sketchbooks that may be attributed to his name. The time has come round at long last to shake these objects free of dust and put in hand any repairs and restorations where these may be needed to make them fit either for market or museum. It has, in other words, become an economic proposition to pay out restorers' and conservators' fees.

It is essential in all this to be under no illusion. The whole area of changing taste and fashion (like the very opinions of art critics themselves) is rich in examples of vagary and myopia. How far anyone may wish to venture forth on these hazardous waters and haul up predictions about where the wayward shifts in wind seem likely to carry present reputations, must depend, in equal measure, on levels of personal self-confidence and a robust bank balance. Yet the moral of it all remains clear. No collector of moderate means should ever try to satisfy an ambition that goes too far beyond the one of simply pleasing himself. Posterity can and certainly should be left to attend to its own devices.

There is, within the field of modern art, one highly contemporary factor that might be seen as setting out to question whether there will ever be any posterity to inherit the cultural present. We live in eschatalogical times — a phrase meaning times when the end of all things is sensed as being imminent. No one alive today can be fully confident that the world, as it is known and experienced, is going to be successful in side-stepping the ultimate crisis and continuing onward into the future. Among the responses of artists to such an apocalyptic level of uncertainty has been the development of ephemeral forms of art, these including 'happenings', which cannot by definition or intention be collected.

It may be felt, with some justification, that we are here starting to look at an area where the plastic arts become trespassers, encroaching on the territory of the dramatic and performing arts, which have been handling the ephemeral quite adequately since the dawn of time. Moreover, it does not follow that the promoters of 'happenings' are necessarily going to come up with anything but a remarkable standard of presentation or performance. Yet the ephemeral does, historically speaking, have a place in the formative years of the modern art movement, especially with the perhaps prophetic experiments of the Dadaists and Surrealists.

There is, it seems, a parable in artistic inspiration to be extracted from the anecdote that concerns the American *avant-garde* painter and photographer Man Ray and his well-known and often illustrated *Object to be Destroyed*. The 'object' itself consisted, quite simply, of a metronome. This carried, attached by a paper-clip to the apex of the pendulum, the cut-out photograph of an eye. It was in 1923 that the work was first seen in an exhibition, and while the artist's declared intention had been to destroy it once the exhibition was over, he could not bring himself to be its executioner when it came to the final test. The 'object' survived until 1957, when a group of students at an exhibition in Paris took its title at face value and reduced it to matchwood. Man Ray lost no time in constructing a replica. On this occasion, he rechristened it *Indestructible Object*. The work survives for the time being and is safely ensconced in a private collection.

Ephemerality and disposability are not, however, the main concerns of the present book. The wider the measure of time that is allowed to slip by, the more complex the relationship grows between artist and ultimate owner. Yet, the reader may well ask, how is it possible ever to describe the owner of a picture as the one who is ultimate? Surely there can never be any such thing as an 'ultimate' home for a work of art, leaving aside the examples of those pictures or sculptures which have, by purchase or bequest, found their way into one of the regional or national art collections. Once they have done this, they have come to be owned by the State and hence, in theory, by a nation at large.

From the viewpoint of other collectors, however, the significance of such works is that they have, in effect, been taken out of the art market. Their valuations have been rendered merely notional. And the very fact of their being spirited out of the market-place enhances the scarcity value of whatever remains. It is a phenomenon that is likely to come to apply to sought-after material of high quality from all periods, and it is one that helps to keep the upward momentum going in art prices in a very direct sort of way.

The fact of the matter is that private collections of pictures continue to be formed, even as private libraries of books continue to be accumulated. The self-same principles apply to collections of works of art as they do for libraries. In due course, the time comes round for their dispersal. It may be that their founder had died or undergone a change of interest. It may simply be that the trouble of caring for and storing a collection has turned into too great a burden to cope with. Nevertheless, as Holbrook Jackson puts it in his majestic study of single-minded book collection, *The Anatomy of Bibliomania*:

. . . many are loath to part from their treasures even
at the end, although they know that unless collections
were dispersed collections could not be made . . . And if
few contemplate the fall of a great tree without regret,
book-lovers may still exult, for . . . when the tree falls
everyone may gather wood . . . Our collections are like
time: they will pass. We are no more, says Anatole France,
than children when they build castles on the seashore:
'the tide sweeps away the sand castles, the auctioneer
disperses the hoarded treasures' . . .

These principles and sentiments are as appropriate for
pictures as they are for books. Even though individual
prints and paintings may remain in a family for a generation,
perhaps over several generations, each of them must, in the
end, find its respective way back to the sale-rooms or dealers'
galleries — back, in other words, into the ever-stirred arena
within which trends of collectability and prices to be looked
for are captured and defined.

'A painting has no intrinsic value' stated the arts correspondent Robert Wraight in his refreshingly sceptical
assessment of the field, *The Art Game*. 'It is a luxury
commodity for which a market is deliberately created and
maintained by financially interested parties who are neither
more nor less noble than the operators of any other legal sort
of market. The market value of art is as artificial as that of
gold or diamonds.'

The world of the dealers may, in fact, be defined as a
gentlemanly jungle. Allowances may need to be made for
individual degrees of ruthlessness, but a jungle it none the
less remains. It will be as well for anyone who sets forth to
venture among the dealers on their home territory to hold
no illusions on this score. But then, it also needs to be said,
this book is not intended to aid those who aspire to being
full-time professional dealers and gallery proprietors. Those
who wish to hew out careers for themselves in these specialized areas of trade must serve their own apprenticeships.
They must, moreover, do so in their own way, accumulating
knowledge and expertise even as a ship on the high seas
accretes barnacles on its hull.

It is important, on the other hand, not to go along
with the impression that the practice of dealing entails an
especially awe-inspiring mystique. For you, the enthusiastic
amateur and part-timer, the possibility of matching the professionals in terms of background knowledge and awareness
of pitfalls is constantly present. It is only necessary for you

to remain clear in your mind about your own area or areas of interest, do your homework by reading and studying the relevant books and up-to-date records of auctions, and take time with your general approach.

Simply to observe and get the feel of the overall scene, is at the outset a leading tactic and a matter for prime importance. To do no more than sit in on a few auctions, absorbing the scene as it progresses from viewing to bidding, can provide you with as richly instructive a store of background experience as you will obtain from any other source. It will also provide you with the opportunity to test out the judgement of your own eyes on the standing or quality of individual pictures. You will find it very instructive to begin comparing your own predictions with the eventual trend revealed in the bidding. You will be, as they say, starting to develop an 'eye'.

It could be that you will even find yourself tempted, during these early days, to make a bid for an item that happens to catch your fancy. Why not, indeed, if you have spotted a picture that strikes a sympathetic chord and maybe seems to be slipping by without attracting too much attention from the dealers? It is quite possible that you will find you have obtained a choice item at a reasonable price. It is also possible that you will discover later, as you come to know more about the ins and outs of the business, that you have, by current reckoning, paid over the odds to secure this particular picture — which was not quite what you thought it was. But nothing is lost. In either event, you will have picked up a snippet of experience that will be to your future advantage. The players must always be prepared, in this game as in any other, to learn as much from their mistakes or miscalculations as they do from their successes.

The sale-rooms have been defined as the arenas of art dealing. This is a view that remains broadly and consistently true. Certainly they have witnessed their share of gladiatorial contests to establish the ownership of certain desirable art works. It may, on the other hand, be more positive to think of them as being the barometers that indicate sea-changes in fashion and taste. Questions of taste and fashion may sometimes seem hard to quantify, but they are, so to speak, ever-present about us in the air. In the end, these are the phenomena that govern the prices at present being paid at auction or charged to clients by dealers' galleries. It follows that a dealer who is aware of having a client or clients lined up and keen to acquire — and so take off his hands — pictures of any particular school or type, or paintings by any particular artist, is going to bid with more determination than a dealer who feels that, if he buys, he is going to have to carry the works as stock for quite a while before it becomes possible to place them with a purchaser. It is such balances of interest as these that help to define the prices paid.

And so the commercial imperative continues to call the tune at every turn, no matter how indignantly we may continue to regret and deplore the fact. It is only after we have managed to steal a march on this imperative that we can start to talk in terms of having got 'a bargain'. And to achieve a bargain, especially in the art-conscious ethos of the present day, we are certainly going to need to foster a pretty shrewd notion of what it is that we are setting out to pursue.

Yet bargains do exist. As another truism has it, there is one to be found in every sale. To spot a bargain, however, you also need to cultivate the instinct for picking a path most carefully across the art world's ever-shifting sands of relative values. You need to develop a clarity in your mind concerning the true nature of the likely reward.

As Robert Wraight laments with some justice in *The Art Game*, the days of innocence are over and done with when it comes to the acquiring and possession of works of art. Pleasure and delight in ownership can, alas, no longer be pursued for their own sake. 'Buying pictures for love of art,' as Mr Wraight says, 'is a thing of the past.'

Whether you are buying to keep or buying to resell makes very little difference. The element of the 'realizable asset' becomes inescapably caught up with our motives and just-ifications. The commercial is always there, however much one may wish it could be otherwise. This fact leads Mr Wraight to paint a somewhat Dickensian portrait of a dealer of the present time — a character for whom it is necessary to learn to look at art:

> with cold, mean, stockbrokerish eyes and be as objective as a butcher sizing up livestock. He will learn to recognize a new fashion in the early stages of gestation and to smell the first whiff of death on a moribund one. He will learn what to buy and when and where to buy it, how much it is worth, how much to pay for it and where and for how much to sell it at any particular time. He will learn not to buy anything simply because he likes it and to buy things he hates if they look like good investments. He will learn the tricks of the trade and how to counter them with

knowledge and cunning of his own and of others whose brains he can pick.

This catalogue of villainies is, quite simply, a consequence of the dramatic upward spirals in fine art values that have taken place during the past few decades. These, in turn, have given the world of art in general a glister in the eye of the public imagination which it never possessed in an earlier age. At the top end of the market, classical masterpieces from various periods as well as masterworks from the modern schools of painting seem never to cease providing fodder for headlines in the popular press as former records for prices are broken, sometimes sensationally, in such metropolitan auction-rooms as Sotheby's and Christie's.

On the other hand, there have been some indications that certain prices did grow to be over-inflated during what came to be regarded as the boom years, which lasted from the 1950s through to the 1970s. As a contrast it was found, during the mid 1980s, that a number of distinguished paintings by artists as illustrious as Cézanne and Van Gogh were suffering the ignomony of being withdrawn from auction after having failed to reach their reserve prices. These setbacks, however, turned out to be only momentary. The glamour attached to the artists' names never ceased to exert its fascination and those who weathered the storms were rewarded by finding the surge of the tide soon turning back in their favour.

Fortunes large enough to keep a family in high comfort for a lifetime have continued to be expended on individual canvases, and the market, by the later 1980s, was clearly restored to its buoyancy. In early 1987, it was announced that the largest of Van Gogh's paintings of sunflowers would be coming up for auction at Christie's in London. It was one of a set of seven that the artist painted in 1888 to decorate the walls of the room he worked in. The auctioneers originally anticipated that the canvas could fetch a sum of over £10 million — this for a work by an artist, we should remind ourselves, who was dismissed and ignored during a lifetime in which he himself sold only one canvas. In the event, when it came to the auction on 30 March (Van Gogh's birthday) *Sunflowers* was knocked down to a bid of £22.5 million, this meaning that, once the buyer's premium had been added, the total price paid came to £24.75 million. This was more than three times the amount for any other picture ever sold at auction, Mantegna's *Adoration of the Magi* having held the previous record at £8.1 million since

Secrets of masterpiece knocked down at Sotheby's for just £33,000

X-rays uncover £6m Titian

by PETER WATSON

PAINTING knocked
n at Sotheby's in
don last April for
000 has been authen-
ed as a Titian worth £6
on.

is claim is made in the
issue of *Apollo*, the

its sale in the London auction
house, where it was valued at
between £20,000 and £30,000
and catalogued as by 'the
studio of Titian.' To the art
world this means that in
Sotheby's opinion it was by an
unknown hand in Titian's

says Mr Christiansen, is t
Titian painted both picture
using the same drawing as
basis for the composition b
introduced variations. T
theme was popular in the
sixteenth century, but a gre
artist would not have wante

Widow's brush-off over £¼m painting

Mary King, 77, was
rday counting the cost
esroom practices which
transformed her £190
ing into a masterpiece
d at £275,000.

her home, The Folly, in
icturesque Dorset village
rne Abbas, widowed Mrs
was ' hopping mad ' about
al which has enriched
s dealers in the chain and
er — the trifling purchase
apart — with only the
oo of 'a present.'

less than six months
oale Carracci's 'A Man in
Act of Drinking' has
plied astronomically in

cn Mrs King's husband
and she moved to a new
there was no longer any

He bought the picture for
£190 when it came up for
auction at Lawrence's saleroom
in Crewkerne last April. Mr
Parker entered the painting in
an auction at Bonham's, the
London saleroom, in July.

Mr Derek Johns, a partner in
the St James's dealers, Harari
and Johns, spotted the work in
the Bonham's catalogue, listed
only as by ' A. Carracci,' which
in the art world code says that
its exact provenance is in
doubt.

It meant that Bonham's — as
well as Mr Parker — had come
to the conclusion that the
picture was a copy or was by
the hand of a follower of
Carracci.

A similar picture, presumed
to be the original, was known to

by PETER WATSON

Mary King and the Carracci she sold for just £190

' it looked horrible, dirty,
neglected, covered in brown

the price up from £800 to more
than £5,000 but it

Northampton, where it was
catalogued as from the Velasquez school.

Mr Johns's sleuthing told him
that it then entered the collection of Sir John Wood in
Suffolk, and then by descent
into the Gage family, who sold
it in 1952, still as from the
school of Velasquez, and it
finished up in Mrs King's
home.

The fact that the painting was
for years mis-catalogued as
being of the Velasquez school is
much more likely, says Mr
Johns, to mean that it is a lost
original than if it had always
been considered a copy or
studio version of a known
work. The

prevented
carefully a
British
convinced
the world

Bologna, Washington and Ne
York.

Professor Posner also say
that the Christ Church pictu
must now be considered
copy.

Mr Johns and Mr Hara
have three American clien
who have agreed to pay the
asking price of £275,000 b
but first they must obtain a
export licence.

Mr Parker is phlegmat
about his £5,000-plus pro
and Bonham's are pleased—
a little nervous — at th
publicity.

As for Mrs King, when to
last week how much th
she was ' bloody annoyed;
of getting over
own and cry.
well do with th

the export licenc
straight away,
e a British galle

Dealers make a killing from Stubbs

Geraldine Norman

ree paintings by George
s, the eighteenth-centu-
inter, have been bought
few hundred pounds in
ncial sales over the past
and resold at Sotheby's
ousands.

r Mark Hancock, a pic-
dealer from west London,
e biggest killing. The
pple Grey Stallion in a
scape" that he bought for
at an R H Ellis sale in
thing last September se-
d £267,948 when it was
by Sotheby's in New York
weeks ago.

r Hancock opted for New
k so that the hurdle of
uiring an export licence
ld be out of the way by the
e it was offered. It was

Detail from "Dapple Grey Stallion in a Landscape"

studies of foxhounds, which
came up at Messenger, May
and Baverstock of Godalming
last October catalogued "English School", sold for £924.

The auctioneers refused to

In Sotheby's London sale of
March 12 one of the foxhound
studies made £34,000 and the
other £54,000. They were
bought by Spink's of King
Street, St James's.

Sotheby's face claim over copy

By Andrew Morgan

A couple whose living-room
painting Sotheby's overvalued
by nearly £40,000 yesterday
said they were considering
seeking compensation from
the auction house for distress.

Sotheby's was given the
painting after Mr Gordon
Melville and his wife, Edith,
had been given a valuation on
the BBC's *Antiques Road-
show*. The auctioneers said
they had carefully examined
the painting and valued it
between £30,000 and £40,000,
advising them to sell in
November.

Earlier, Mr David Mason,
resident expert on the BBC's
Antiques Roadshow, had valued the painting, which the
couple called "The Hare in the
Snow", at up to £50,000 during
a recording on July 9. He said
it was the work of the Swedish
painter Bruno Liljefors.

Mr Melville signed a con-
tract on August 19 allowing
Sotheby's to sell the painting.

Hearing nothing for weeks,
Mr Meville telephoned Miss
Cherry Kisch, of Sotheby's
nineteenth century art department, who said there were
doubts on authenticity.

Mr Alex Apsis, of Sothe-
by's, told him last week he had
located the original in a private Swedish coillection and
Mr Melville's painting, dated
about 1900, was a copy worth
£500.

In a letter, Mr Apsis said
the initial valuation was a
"first impression". Mr Melville said: "We were dev-
astated." Sotheby's said
yesterday: "We are not infal-
lible and it must be a mega-
disappointment but if our
expertise had not been so
good, then a fake could have
been released on to the art
market".

The BBC said last night
that the show's producers were
disappointed. Mr Mason said
it was his first big mistake in
10 years. Mr Christopher
Lewis, the producer, described
the painting as a "brilliant
fake".

HE TIMES TUESDAY NOVEMBER 5 1985

Sale room

'Lost' Rossetti drawing sold

By Geraldine Norman, Sale Room Correspondent

w's paid £28,600 (estimate
00-£8,000) at Phillips yester-
for a pen and ink drawing of
Morris, William Morris's
by Dante Gabriel Rossetti.
rent theme in Rossetti's work,
itry face with billowing hair,
drawing of her reclining on a
has not been seen by the public
it was exhibited at the New
ery in 1897.

was brought into Phillips by a
who assumed that he had a
ographic reproduction or en-
ing, not the real thing. It had
at Christie's in 1883 for £11.

nother much-admired discovery
the pastel portrait of a
nned gentleman by Francis
s dating from about 1750
h sold for £17,600 (estimate
00-£8,000) to Colnaghi's. Few
els have survived in good
ition but this was an exception.
ad come to Rossetti's work,
an in Bristol whose family had
d it for some time.

he sale of English drawings and
rcolours was outstandingly
ssful, reflecting the wide-
ad collector interest in the field
the high quality of the
ings on offer. A new auction
record was set for the work of

Thomas Shotter Boys when his
townscape, "Rue des Prêtes, St
Germain l'Auxerrois, Paris," made
£46,200 (estimate £12,000-
£18,000). It is dated 1830 and was
bought by Andrew Wyld, a London
dealer.

He also paid £35,200 (estimate
£10,000-£15,000) for John Robert
Cozens's "Between Salerno and
Eboli", another auction price record
for the artist. The extensive view
with a big pine tree and a palm in
the foreground is one of the
watercolours made for the collector,
Sir William Beckford.

It was included in the Beckford
sale of 1805 when it was described
as "very fine, a chaste and beautiful
drawing, tinted in a sweet silvery
tone". With its soft grey-blue tones,
so it remains today. The sale
totalled £338,200 with 3 per cent
unsold.

Sotheby's found that nineteenth-
century paintings are as difficult to
sell in Amsterdam as in London or
New York with an auction totalling
£285,043 and 30 per cent unsold.
The Dutch pictures brought the top
prices with an Arnoldus Bloemers,
"Still life of Flowers", selling for
143,750 guilders (estimate 50,000-
80,000 guilders) or £33,430 to a
London dealer.

'Lost' Turner on show

Mr Julian Agnew, managing
director of Agnew's, inspecting
an uncatalogued watercolour
by J. M. W. Turner, which he
discovered in the United
States.

The signed picture, entitled
"The Chapter House,
Hereford", will be on show at
Agnew's 115th Exhibition of
Watercolours and Drawings
which opens today at their
gallery in Old Bond Street,
London.

The painting was originally
thought to be of Glastonbury
Abbey but Mr Andrew Wilton,
curator of the Turner Collection at the Clore Gallery, links
it to a pencil sketch

Cotes's fine paste
gentleman,

1985. And lest it should be thought that here was a freak result prompted by the extraordinary popularity of the sunflower image, eight months later, in November, Sotheby's auctioned *Irises*, another fine but less well-known Van Gogh, for $53.9 million (about £30 million).

For a whole variety of reasons, the overall trend in the art market has continued to be one of an upward mobility. This progression is bound, in its way, to be self-perpetuating, especially since it is happening in an age when national currencies continue to a greater or lesser extent to pursue their own inflationary spirals. In these circumstances, the purchase of a work of art may be viewed as a haven in which to invest either a small, moderate or sizeable slice of capital. The work itself becomes, so to speak, a capsule wherein the investment entrusted to it will yield a return both equivalent to and competitive with rates available from other sources of investment over the same period.

In Britain, during the 1970s, the British Rail Pension Fund included the purchase of works of art among its investment portfolios, making an investment of between £40 and £50 million and providing an example of an institution playing the art market directly in parallel with the Stock Exchange. In a similar way, many rich collectors include art portfolios among their range of business interests. They take note of advice offered by stockbrokers who specialize in this area and, so to speak, hedge their bets by ensuring that their wealth is spread over a broad range of possibilities. Side by side with these there exists a world-wide network of national, state and university art galleries and institutes, all in constant competition with the mega-rich among individual collectors in their efforts to add to the scope and representativeness of the treasures they hold in their magnificent storehouses.

From all of this it may be seen how, where works of merit, rarity and genuine provenance are concerned (the hazards of false attribution and skilled forgery are constantly lying in wait to ambush the unwary), there seems no good reason to anticipate that the bottom is going to drop out of any particular market. All such considerations may, however, seem remote from the well-spring of vision, craftsmanship and intention that led a particular artist to create a specific work of art. Whenever the notions of the cultural and financial values of art become separated from each other, there are bound to be distortions in the form of over – and under – estimations. If, in the long run, any direct correlation between a percentage return on interest and the market

Sunflowers, the Van Gogh painting which fetched in excess of £22 million, being examined by Peter Rose of Christie's prior to the auction in March 1987.

price of works of art turns out to be a bogus notion, then the spectacle of art extracting its revenge is going to seem to many to be tipping the scales of justice in the right direction.

Those who feel that the equating of interest returns and art values is a fallacious exercise would claim that the forces at work are far too random to justify coming to such self-confident conclusions. In the view of the noted New York art dealer, Eugene Victor Thaw, expressed in an article in *The Times* of 25 September 1982, all such speculation always 'was nonsensical':

Works of art are not like diamonds [or] gold bars . . . You cannot trade in Monet or Matisse commodity futures . . . Only art is collected, in the proper sense of the word, not for its utility or as a repository of value, but for the pleasure owning it affords.

When the British Rail Pension Fund came to start to return some of its investments to the market-place during the course of 1987, there were areas of triumphant vindication (antique silver showing a healthy appreciation) but others of disappointment (a Stubbs painting failing to reach its reserve price). It is not, however, a concern of the present book to chart the scales of values and reputations as these have progressed for all the great names from Leonardo to Picasso. This is an obsessive preoccupation, and one that may safely be left in other hands. If ever the work of some established front-rank artist, whose name redounds down the ages, does turn up incognito in a sale, then this is, it needs to be said, an event of considerable rarity.

There is no doubting the fact that the occasional unrecognized Poussin does lurk somewhere in a cellar. In the same way, an attic just as doubtless contains a mislaid Constable oil-painting. There such paintings are, draped in unseemly layers of dust and cobwebs. But make no mistake about it, your chances of stumbling across either one of them, or any of the dozens of equivalents, are very remote.

It does happen, of course. It happened in 1986 with an unrecognized Stubbs of a dapple-grey stallion, sold at a provincial auction for £562 and subsequently for £267,948 in New York. And which of us would wish to be in the position of the elderly widow who, in 1985, saw the painting she put in a sale and sold for £190 realize £275,000 after it had spent six months passing through a chain of dealers? In this case, what was thought to have been only a copy of a painting by Annibale Carracci of a man drinking from a glass was in due course authenticated by a leading art historian as an original.

There is no reason, of course, why you should not set out to make the rediscovery of lost masterpieces by famous artists your hobby. All we are saying is that you should only do so provided you remain clear in your mind that the likelihood is strong that you will finish your days without scoring a single success. Yes, we can see it is true that people do come by such treasures through extraordinary or bizarre chains of circumstance, but we also know that the odds against it happening are long indeed. The possibility should, for all practical purposes, be discounted and relegated to the realm of wish-fulfilment — not quite as remote as the chances of winning a fortune in a lottery or through the football pools, perhaps, but very nearly so. If it should happen to you, consider it to be among life's bonuses.

This is the point where you find yourself hesitating on the threshold to an unfamiliar territory — one which is a more common preserve for the dealers and auctioneers. Does the prospect seem to you somewhat daunting? It is only natural, if you have never attended an auction before, that you should feel you are about to go through a new, even an alien experience. Allow your nerves to settle quietly. You will find that it takes you no time whatever to begin to pick up the gist and the mechanics of all that goes on in these surrounds.

2
THE
SALES
ARENA

If it has been at all possible to do so, you should have obtained a copy of the auctioneer's catalogue several days beforehand. A margin of time in which to give the publication some study will be invaluable. If this has been impossible, however, then make a point of picking up a catalogue as soon as you arrive before the auction. On another point of principle, arriving as early as possible before any bidding commences is also important. You certainly do not want to have to rush and skimp at any stage of the proceedings. You are going to need as much leisurely elbow room as you can muster. In this margin of space and time, you will be able to circulate, observe and put to the test the mixture of intuitive feelings and hard knowledge that you are beginning to accumulate, and then match this against the pictures on display.

From the outset, start to compare the written descriptions in the catalogue with what you actually find before your eyes. Use your discretion to notice unobtrusively how the dealers themselves approach the pictures and then move in to centre their examinations on those that alert their interest. Observe how they pay special attention to painted surfaces, markings and signatures among other details; and how they perhaps lift down a picture from its hanging, so as to turn it about and peer at the way it is set in its frame and check the wood for structural soundness; or examine the texture of a canvas on its stretcher; or even, if it is an oil, rub a finger, primed with spit, in a brisk circle over a small portion of the painting's surface.

STANDING
ON THE
THRESHOLD

You should not expect to be able to eavesdrop on much in the way of conversation at this stage. There will be a general atmosphere of restraint as all those present appear to

23

be keeping their thoughts and counsel very much to themselves. The chance to eavesdrop should come later, but even so, despite the lack of verbal comment, it should by now be growing clear which pictures are the ones in the running to draw a lion's share of attention. With the moment for the start of the auction drawing ever closer, position yourself strategically. You will want to be seated at an angle that allows you to see everything that is going on without the need to crane your neck or look back over your shoulder. Bear in mind that pointedly looking around or behind you to see who is bidding is considered a breach of etiquette in dealers' circles.

From this point on, you should be fully alert to the styles of bidding favoured by individual buyers. And individualism may indeed be seen to come into its own in this matter. Notice how the auctioneer responds to his clients' idiosyncracies, whatever form they take. A bid may be registered by an emphatic nod of the head, by raising skyward a folded pair of spectacles, by slightly tilting upward a tightly rolled catalogue, or by other signs so discreet as to seem practically invisible. The auctioneer will miss none of them. There is probably no mode or eccentricity of bidding that he has not come across in the course of his career. One is put in mind of the auction attended by Jonathan Raban and described in his book *Coasting* — an auction not of pictures but of fish, though the self-same principles apply:

> Two merchants were bidding against each other. Both had pipes — one a meerschaum, the other a briar. To bid, each man wagged his pipe a fraction of an inch with his teeth. Meerschaum, briar, meerschaum, briar. Neither was alight. The bowls titupped along in an easy foxtrot rhythm until the briar went doggo at sixteen pounds.

The spectacles offered by auction-rooms everywhere are naturally highly diverting, especially to a newcomer. But you should not allow this fact to deflect attention from the main task in hand. As soon as bidding begins, you must start meticulously noting in the margin of your catalogue the price achieved by each item as it is knocked down. In doing this, you will be starting to build up a record that will provide you with some interesting comparisons to look back over later when you have the time free. In the meantime, keep a keen eye on how accurate your own initial hunches on the value of the goods on offer are turning out to be in practice.

As each item is sold, the auction-room attendants will

remove it to the back office, where the actual business transactions are themselves completed. In due course, the walls and display panels will be starting to look sadly denuded. Take this as your signal, since the end of the auction is drawing near, to resort to the saloon bar of the nearest public-house and get yourself fixed up with a drink. Opportunities for eavesdropping should now be here in plenty as dealers, with their business colleagues and associates, gather into groups about the bar and tables.

The tensions and competitiveness of the sale-room are now behind them. They will therefore feel ready to unwind and launch into shop talk and gossip about the various aspects of the sale. Topics are likely to range from the standards, desirability and collectability of the works that have been included to the prices fetched and how these compare with those of other recent occasions; and they may well spill over into more general aspects of the art market and the tendencies it seems to be developing at the present time.

If you have the chance to create an opening and enter into a casual conversation or two during this period of aftermath and assessment, then do not be shy of doing so. You may find that the exercise brings you some useful insights into how this particular sale has looked from the general standpoint of the trade. On the other hand, do not expect to hear too much in the way of good news. Art dealers are very like farmers: whichever way the climate goes, it always goes against them.

For you, however — still occupying a position at such an early point in the process of putting down a foundation on which to base future ventures — there are two requirements which are paramount. First, you should have started to develop a clear-eyed idea of exactly what it is that constitutes 'quality'. Secondly, you should have consciously tried to begin directing your ideas and energies towards the challenge of always going, not for bargains as such, but *after the best obtainable* — and this rule applies irrespective of the period, style or medium that you have under consideration.

QUESTIONS OF QUALITY

Having come as far as this, it should in fact be a fair assumption that you are beginning to piece together at least a preliminary sense of where your personal sympathies, enthusiasms and predilections are liable in due time to carry you. These conscious responses are the ones that are bound to coalesce into your personal areas of specialization.

It could be that you feel drawn towards the works of important local or regional artists who lived earlier in the present century. Alternatively, you might find yourself developing an enthusiasm for hunting or sporting scenes; or perhaps it is maritime subjects, in a broad sense, that are beginning to seize your interest. On the other hand, it may be that you are falling in love with Regency or early Victorian miniatures; or simply with *genre* pictures in general. (The term *genre*, incidentally, means nothing more in this context than pictures which illustrate people going about their everyday activities in the course of their domestic or working lives.)

Having said all that, it could be that you have never intended going too far beyond the simple intention of pleasing yourself. 'I think,' you may say, 'that I'd really like to stay free from the troublesome complication of having to take into account off-the-cuff speculations. All I want to be able to do is hang on my walls pictures which happen to possess a certain happy, personal sort of appeal.' Excellent, if this is the case. You are not going to have any great need for the advice being given here. But then neither will there seem to be much of a prospect in view for you to develop any real connoisseurship of the arts. To do that, your ambitions will need to extend beyond the limits of mere serendipity. You are going to wish to be well placed to explore the pleasures that lie in informed appreciation. There is no alternative here to making sure that you carry, clearly engraved in your mind, a comprehensive set of guide-lines.

In the whole of the past and the future history of art, it must be the *quality* of the original artistic talent, and its control over its techniques, that will produce a picture capable of holding its own over time. However our subjective views of what constitutes that essential quality may shift and alter, only a picture with such antecedents can come to represent a truly lasting pleasure. In other words, excellence is everything. This applies even if you are thinking exclusively in terms to collect and not to resell: the same question of excellence still comes into play. How otherwise are you going to be sure that your collection remains something that is worth paying more than a passing mention to and which your heirs will be pleased to inherit? Similarly, if you are buying with the idea of reselling at some unspecified time in the future, then it can only be the degree of subtlety, strength and skill present in your collection that is going to maintain the value of your original outlay — let alone justify the time and trouble you went to in putting it together.

The fundamental test of a good, worthwhile picture may be said to be defined by the question: will it continue to live and breathe once it has been hung on the wall? It is, believe

Two examples of *genre* paintings: (Above) *Reading the Exeter Gazette* by James Leakey (1775-1865). Oil on canvas. 1838. (Left) *The Woodcutters* by Thomas Barker of Bath (1769-1847). Oil on canvas c. 1790.

it or not, possible for a picture to die. A picture has done so, in fact, from the moment it fails to continue putting out the sense of freshness and unexpectedness that its owner originally found attractive. In this case it has failed, to put it another way, to stand up to the test of becoming known through daily familiarity. We might, in fact, evoke this as a graphic illustration of time being the great selector.

It could, however, be said accusingly that raising the in-the-end intangible questions of quality and taste promises only to take us into territory where every opinion anyone could express remains wide open to debate. Yet it also stays consistently true that, to appreciate excellence, the eye needs to become both cultivated and educated. Only after this has been achieved does the eye become capable of phasing itself in with those more instinctive reactions of viewing a picture as something to evoke the response, 'Ah, now there is one I like.' Conversely, the appeal of a painting that is little more than a demonstration of sheer technique, and which has nothing much more to be said for it, can pall quite quickly. Perhaps, in the end, the most that may be said is that a painting turns out well when it has been created in that alchemical area where artistic craftsmanship and the tricks of the trade merge mysteriously with the far less easily definable element of vision.

LOOKING
AND
LEARNING

So far as educating the eye goes, it needs to be thoroughly emphasized that you can hardly spend too much time over simply looking, and looking again and again, at pictures of all kinds and from every age. There are various ways in which you can set about doing this. The auction-rooms are themselves, of course, places where you can look at pictures. Additionally, you should create every opportunity you can to drop in casually at dealers' galleries. You can do this either in your own locality or further afield, if you happen to be travelling about for either business or personal reasons.

You should, moreover, familiarize yourself with whatever works of art are represented in the collections of your county or regional art galleries and museums. These may be on show, or they may be tucked away in the archives — exhibition space is often at a premium, especially in this day and age. You may have to ask museum or gallery staff whether you can see whatever there is in the reserve collections. And you should certainly not neglect to become broadly aware of those artists who are currently at work in your region and of the styles of work they follow. This applies even if you do not include any aspect of the present-day artistic schools among your personal preferences.

These are all among the important routes that lie open to you, and which will enable you to build up a wide background knowledge at the same time as you develop your technique for looking at pictures. All other considerations aside, the fun, constructiveness and instructiveness contained in this pastime, activity or hobby — define it how you may — can only be enhanced when you are able to back it up with a sense of the past and present unfolding of the history of art. You will certainly need to equip yourself with an idea of how styles have changed, and how the subjects favoured by painters have altered from period to period. There is no other way in which you can make yourself fully alert to the problems of following the twists and turns in the changing patterns of taste among clients and patrons.

Moreover, if it is true that you cannot do too much looking at pictures, then it is equally true that you cannot do too much consulting and reading of books, both on art history and specific artists, and of catalogues of major exhibitions and other similar material. There are a number of books that you are going to find indispensable when you come to buy or sell paintings on any serious basis (and these are listed on pages 50-1 of Chapter 3). There are certain other books that you are going to find helpful more for their value as background reading and for the way they can lead you to study the subject in increasing depth (some suggestions for these being given in the selected reading list on page 147).

The main point being laboured here, however, is that you should not look to find easy ways round the volumes of material that face you. You need to read every book on art on which you can lay your hands — and especially those that have a bearing on the areas that you may already feel are going to be the ones to constitute your particular interests.

Here is probably as good a place as any at which to pause to define what is generally understood by the phrase 'original work of art'. Naturally, a piece of sculpture or a hand-thrown pot or vase may both qualify, but, equally clearly, these would not fall within the scope of the present text. When talking about pictures, the 'original work of art' may consist of a painting done either in oils, or in water-colour, or in gouache or acrylic. An innovation from more recent times means that we should also place collage under this heading, a collage being made up of a miscellany of materials (on occasions aiming for three-dimensional effects)

THE 'ORIGINAL WORK OF ART'

mixed in with any or all of the more traditional media. An original work may also consist of a sketch or drawing, either in charcoal, pencil or ink, or in pastel or wax crayon.

Prints also fall under the heading of 'original works', subject to certain conditions and circumstances. A print, in this case, is quite distinct from a 'reproduction'. It is an artwork in its own right, produced by any method that makes it possible to run off an edition of a few or many copies, all of which are capable of displaying a consistent quality. The most commonly encountered printmaking processes include etching, lithography, screen-printing, aquatinting, woodcuts or linocuts; or combinations of two or more of these various printmaking methods.

The edition in which a print is produced will usually be guaranteed as carrying a limit of, say, 50, 100 or 150 copies, since, it is only logical to add, an edition that was reproduced without limit could hold little appeal or value for collectors. Each individual print then produced for sale will need to carry the autograph of the artist and a specification to indicate how many prints the edition consists of and what its series number is within the edition. The code '36/100', for instance, will inform you that here is print No. 36 out of a run or edition restricted to no more than 100 copies.

The print has, in modern times especially, been seen as a means of 'democratizing' art, since it offers the public an opportunity to buy original work (often by quite well-known artists) at economic prices. At the same time, it gives artists the chance to see their work disseminated among broader sections of the population than would otherwise be possible, and this in itself represents an attractive consideration.

Prints from earlier periods, and especially those which show local topographical scenes, geographical or architectural features, may also have their value — as may printed period or antique maps. So, alas, do prints removed from rare books which have been 'cannibalized' — as the term has it for the greedy, barbaric practice of breaking up fine examples of illustrated antiquarian books so as to utilize their finely printed plates and amplify the profit margins obtainable on resale.

A word of warning needs to be heeded by the novice where prints are concerned. The whole area of prints and maps is scattered and undermined by many pitfalls. The questions of value and scarcity (or of their lowness in value and common availability) bring us to the point where we run into special areas of knowledge in which it is only too easy to be deceived by one's perceptions. The tyro in the field is therefore to be firmly advised to leave well alone initially. He or she should hold back until such time as a patina of background has accumulated, and with it a feeling of confidence that it is possible to recognize what is being looked at for what it truly is.

During the whole of this period of gathering impressions and knowledge, you will have been continuing to gain insights into the psychological workings of auction-rooms and their main denizens, the dealers. You may well have begun to conclude that this is an absorbing enough study in itself. The time, however, is arriving — perhaps has already arrived — when you can begin to put some of your observations to practical use. In other words, you should actually be starting to think about meeting a dealer on his home ground, and taking the plunge of offering to sell him something you have acquired at auction.

THE 'VISITING-CARD'

Have you as yet chanced your arm and pursued a bid through to its conclusion? If not, you should now go to an auction with that purpose firmly in mind. As you allow an appraising eye to pass over the range of pictures on offer on the walls, be attentive to watch for an example that looks capable of serving at least one turn as your *entrée* or 'visiting-card'. By this we mean something that is good enough and interesting enough to show to a gallery owner with a fair measure of confidence. You want him to be able to take you seriously, after all. You are therefore poised to enter the game in earnest and about to gain some first-hand experience of the excitement of taking a gamble and backing your hunch.

We have already said that all of this may seem a shade reminiscent of picking a horse to back at the racecourse. The great advantage in this case is that you find yourself, among these pictures, on far more solid ground as you make a study of form, as the racing fraternity put it. It does, of course, remain true that you take a risk with your money each time you buy. But, in contrast with the racecourse scene, you are here in a situation where you can minimize the risk to whatever stake you may be putting forward. At the same time, the release of adrenalin that comes into play and the general buzz of excitement that you feel can easily reach comparable levels, even though the way you show it needs to be far less demonstrative.

You do, however, need to ask yourself what the nature of such a picture will be — which one among those on display is most likely to catch the eye of the gallery proprietor (let us say his name is Mr Aster) on whom you are planning to call. Out of all the possible subjects, in other words, the question remains which are the ones most likely to prompt him into treating you as someone to whom he is prepared to give a morsel of time out of his day, irrespective of whether or not he happens to be buying at the moment?

On this occasion, the best tactic to recommend is that you should concentrate on singling out a pleasing, presentable water-colour. At least, when it comes to water-colours, you can remain reasonably sure that they are what they are stated to be in the auctioneer's catalogue. The fact of the matter is that water-colours are rarely felt to be worth the trouble of faking. This is not to say, it hardly needs stating, that any reputable auctioneer would ever knowingly include a fake or a wrongly attributed work in a sale; but questions of attribution and provenance can become, at times, exceedingly complex. This is why you should go for a water-colour at this stage, knowing that such a picture is likely to be a genuine representative of its period. In this way, you will safely circumnavigate the potentially embarrassing trap of being told that an item that looked like an interesting original is more probably the work of some copyist or even a forger.

As you start to mark down the possibilities in the catalogue, never lose sight of the first rule: that whatever you buy ought to be something that you would not at all object to have gracing your walls at home. Look especially at landscapes, and, for preference, at those that feature either a few human figures or else some sort of animal life. A sellable landscape needs to show a sunny day and to convey a bright colourful atmosphere.

An alternative choice could be provided by a seascape. It will need to be a lively example. There should be yachts and shipping going about their business, and a clear indication in the way the painting is executed of whether the day is a calm or choppy one at sea. But, whatever the subject of the picture you finally secure, it should obviously be in a good, clean state and be mounted in a suitable and structurally sound frame.

In all your auction-going, never neglect to take along your packet of sandwiches and your flask of coffee. You may find that there are many long periods of waiting ahead of you before the lot or lots in which you are interested come under the auctioneer's hammer. Do not omit, either, to read carefully through all the small print that covers the auctioneer's conditions of sale. You will find these listed in the sale catalogue. You must also check on whether the auctioneer requires any client making a purchase to a value above a certain limit to provide a banker's reference. If you have not hitherto made a point of introducing yourself to the auctioneer, making sure that you know his name and he yours, you should certainly do so now.

By this stage, it seems likely that you will have reached some sort of decision on the personal style of bidding you intend to adopt. Whether you are planning to go for something in the line of a flamboyant flourish, or to take up one of the more discreet types of signal, is all going to depend on the leanings of your own personality and general inventiveness. One thing is certain. You should by now be safely over the hurdle of the classic fear of those who say they would never go to an auction in case they batted an eyelid at the wrong moment and found themselves the owner of an unwanted monstrosity. You will have observed for yourself that this myth does not really reflect the way in which auctions operate.

Perhaps, before we close this chapter, we should also say a few words to bring dealers into their proper perspective. They do not, for instance, usually sport horns and tails. Nor are they invariably monsters of avarice. Experience will demonstrate that they consist, as a rule, of charming, cultivated and courteous individuals. They are pleasant enough personalities, in other words, with whom to become engaged in conversation, and they make as good acquaintances and friends to have as anyone in any other walk in life.

Nevertheless, in every dealing you have with a dealer, there is a certain reservation to be securely borne in mind. Under no circumstances should you allow yourself to be lulled into forgetting that, for every dealer who exists in the world, matters of acquaintanceship and friendship fall neatly within one of life's compartments, questions of business within another. Only in the most rare of circumstances will sentiment be allowed to spill simultaneously over on to both sides of the partition.

To say this implies no moral criticism; it only points to a phenomenon that might be defined, by the observant dealer watcher, as a built-in instinctive survival pattern common to the species. The expectation that this is so will stand you in good stead as you set out along the path to becoming a buyer, collector and disposer of pictures. It is a route that will allow you to explore many opportunities for pleasure and profit, the two motives intermingling as you chart your progress.

3
SOURCES
OF
INFORMATION

THE
HORSE'S
MOUTH

Mr Aster maintains his showrooms in one of the town's smarter streets. The shops here alternate with business premises, and the shops themselves are, on the whole, the type offering a rather superior class of goods. Moreover, the district is partly residential, and the side-streets, with their houses quite smartly done up and maintained these days, indicate a local population that could hardly be described as on the breadline.

Certain of Mr Aster's regular clients may well live in the neighbourhood, and casual callers at the showrooms may account for a modest proportion of the sales his firm achieves. The foundations for his business, however, exist on a far broader base than could be provided by an exclusively local clientele. How otherwise could the business ever have grown into the success it undoubtedly is today, to judge from the well-equipped and well-stocked galleries?

The range of clients who buy from Mr Aster originates, in fact, from a wide geographical area in terms of counties, even of countries. Their numbers will include dealers in the trade as well as individual collectors whose interests are all meticulously recorded on files or indexes. Each of these clients will receive regular mailings of Mr Aster's price lists and catalogues, while he, for his part, will know precisely who among them is, at this particular moment, looking for the work of any particular artists or schools of painting. The clients are also quite likely to include a number of interior decorators. These professionals are forever on the look-out for pictures that might be utilized as decorative furnishings for premises where they are under contract to do them up in various styles — hotels, restaurants, inns, luxury apartments.

Whoever the people may be who go to make up his clientele, however, Mr Aster's ideas on what he is able to sell, either through personal contact or by display on the walls or in the racks of his gallery, will be clear and precise. In other words, he knows the kind of material that will give him the reasonably fast turnover on a proportion of his stock that he has to look for if his business is to stay afloat. The stock he holds will not therefore be, in any sense, a random or jackdaw gathering.

Everything on offer in Mr Aster's gallery will have been

carefully considered from one angle or another. If he should happen to purchase an item of merit when he knows it could remain in stock for quite some time, then it will also have been part of his calculation that such a picture is likely, in due course, to find an appreciative buyer; neither will it have diminished in value in any real terms by the time it is sold.

As you make your entrance into Mr Aster's domain, carefully bearing your modest treasure — your 'visiting-card' — for him to inspect, try to keep yourself as alert as possible to the work he has on display. As you move through the showroom, remember that impressions are important. It is also important that you should get to speak to Mr Aster himself. If an assistant or secretary suggests you leave your picture for Mr Aster to look at and assess at his leisure, do not allow yourself to be fobbed off. Politely decline and ask if you could make an appointment to call back at a more convenient time. Remember that it is not, at this stage, a matter of vital importance whether or not Mr Aster actually buys what you have to sell. The main purpose of this stage of the proceedings is to take the chance of engaging a dealer in conversation and discovering his particular needs in the present state of the market.

Even if Mr Aster speaks dismissively of the picture you produce to show to him, there is no need to take this to heart. The initial investment will continue to be fully justified by the information and experience it is bringing your way and adding to your as yet meagre store of knowledge. Follow up any advantage you have been able to gain by showing as great an interest as you can muster in his present stock. The less naïve you strike him as being, the more seriously he is going to treat you. Ask if he will kindly allow you to browse through the racks or portfolios of undisplayed pictures and prints. Make mental notes especially of the range of prices he seems to be able to command from his vantage point in the art market.

But now, as he shrewdly and knowingly casts an eye over your 'visiting-card', Mr Aster may comment that, yes, it really is quite a nice picture. On the other hand, he may add, it does seem to be the work of some talented amateur. He himself has no knowledge of the artist's name. In telling you this, he is telling you in the politest way possible that you have made a basic mistake where the present picture is concerned. *You have gone for the work of an artist whose name is unrecorded in the books of sales records.*

The importance of this lesson cannot be over-emphasized. If you are buying pictures to resell at a profit, and not simply to please a whim of the moment, then it needs to be possible to establish the identity of an artist in those works of reference that are generally regarded by the trade as being the essential guides. (For the section on essential reference books, see page 50 below.)

PRELIMINARY OUTLAY You should, during the course of the initial weeks or months, be taking out subscriptions to as many relevant auctioneers' catalogues and dealers' price lists as you possibly can, the metropolitan ones (Christie's and Sotheby's) as well as the provincial ones. This will greatly increase your familiarity with the art market, its subtle and not so subtle drifts, and the kind of work and the names of artists that turn up at auction sales. Collectors' magazines (see pages 46-8 below) are further items which fully justify paying a subscription, since the articles and details of sale-room activities they contain can provide you with invaluable background guides for assessing current trends or fresh collectable discoveries. Your accumulation of background knowledge does, indeed, need to be an ever-onward process. To operate successfully in this field, you need to know all its latest ups, downs and about-turns.

Talk of subscriptions gives us a cue to the reminder, if such is needed, that a certain outlay is essential before you are even into the preliminary stages of exploring and financing the operation. This is something that applies whether the basis on which the operation is to be performed is spare-time or full-time. Over and beyond the subscriptions to price lists, catalogues and magazines, the prospective picture buyer should also give some thought to investing in a collection of books to build up a basic reference library. Moreover, there will be travelling expenses between home, sale-rooms and dealers' galleries to be considered, not to mention the costs of personal subsistence whenever you happen to be away from home.

As soon as all these requirements are taken into account, it becomes clear that certain sums, representing 'operating capital', will need to be set aside to place you on a solid platform for the conducting of your enterprise. The prices you pay at auction to acquire your preliminary stock-in-trade will then need to leave you with a certain margin of profit when you come to resell. This profit margin should, of course, be one that will cover your overheads (your running costs) and leave you with a surplus.

It is this surplus that you should ideally be able to divert into the creation of the fund out of which you can plan to finance your own collection of artists for whose work you have a special place on your walls and a fondness in your heart. Never should you forget that, since you will be obtaining these works at auction prices, you will be assembling your collection on the basis of an outlay that may be described as fair and reasonable.

At this point, it seems as well to return to basic considerations and establish some clear thinking on what it is that we are setting out to achieve.

OPTIONS AND OBJECTIVES

There are, in fact, three possible ways in which to start out in the business of collecting pictures, the first option being to go in search of old ladies, the attics, broom-cupboards or cellars of whose houses may contain pictures which have been in their families as long as they can remember. But the problems attached to looking for old ladies and persuading them to part with their treasures may well be quite considerable. You may, in fact, spend the rest of your life searching for one such old lady, or you may be lucky and, in this way, pick up something very special for a mere song.

But even if we leave the ethics of this kind of approach on one side, it is still no way in which to conduct a business. It takes us, what is more, into the grey and disagreeable area of the 'knockers' — those shady characters who knock on doors and ask householders if they have anything they want to get rid of for cash, in the hope of taking off their hands various goods at a fraction of their disposable values. Such acts come under the heading of fraudulent practice, and old ladies today are considerably shrewder and more knowing than perhaps they used to be about what their antique possessions are likely to be worth. They may even have had them valued, and you may, quite justifiably, find your intrusion being reported to the police.

The second possible approach is to go to the art galleries and antique shops with the object of buying direct from the dealers themselves. The great and most obvious disadvantage of this option is that anything you buy from this source will already have the dealer's profit topping up the price he is charging you. He will, in other words, sell to you, particularly if you are a newcomer on the scene, at about the same price he would charge anybody else who happened to wander casually into his shop. If you have made yourself known, and if you are lucky, he may well knock off a small percentage, but always remember that he may, as it were, have sensed an idiot approaching and already have rounded it up just that little bit more.

The fact remains that, if you are hoping to get a business started, then this still gives you no basis on which to set about it. This does not, of course, mean to say that, if you are specializing in the collection of certain pictures or artists and happen to spot an example you like in a gallery or antique shop, you should not buy it if the price seems a fair one. That is another matter, and one which has to do specifically with collecting. It has nothing whatever to do with conducting business, and this is one distinction that should be clear-cut from the outset.

The implication of all this is that we are left with only one way in which the beginner can hope to rely on being able to make some money at the same time as enjoying himself: by attending auctions. Auctions are not, however, the be-all and end-all of the process. If you are really serious about creating a foothold for yourself in the art business, then you must now be prepared to set aside a lengthy period — say, between six and nine months — in which to undertake preparatory work. On no account should you launch yourself in earnest until this is behind you.

During this period of essential groundwork, you will be visiting as many art galleries as you can possibly fit in to your schedule. The galleries that you are able to visit may depend on where you happen to live in the British Isles. (A list of main public galleries and art collections is given in Appendix II, starting on page 157). If you live within reach of London, then go to the National Gallery, the Tate Gallery, and the Victoria and Albert Museum. If you live at any great distance from London, then it will pay you to plan a visit to the metropolis and spend a few days sightseeing in the national collections if that is at all possible during this preparatory period. You should also periodically make visits to those commercial art galleries that are accessible to you in your region and take a look around; and keep an eye open for posters or notices in the local press of exhibitions that could be of interest to you. Your local regional arts association will be another source of information on current exhibitions in the district.

As you do all of this, bear it positively in mind that you are still only a beginner, that you are in the earliest phase of starting a hobby or a business, that you are not a millionaire, and that the only work which is going to lie within your reach (and which should be the focus of your attention) is nineteenth-century and early twentieth-century English art. This is not to say that, if something from the eighteenth century presents you with a chance to buy, then you should ignore it. It is only to say that your concentration should be mainly on the Victorian and Edwardian periods, and perhaps on the minor schools of art that flourished during the 1920s and 1930s. It is here that the main possibilities will lie for you and the limited resources you have at your disposal.

It goes without saying that, in these areas as much as in any other, pictures all the time become more expensive to buy. Again, however, it should be borne in mind that it is the work of so-called minor artists that is, as a rule, going to be engaging your attention. The names which come your way will not, on the whole, be those that are regarded as 'major'. You will not, in the normal way, be handling pictures by those artists who are represented in the leading national permanent collections. Nevertheless, as you look at pictures in those collections, you should, without exception, be studying the work of all artists from all periods — for your pleasure and relaxation as much as for your education. While you may not need to anticipate that you will have the work of any major figure passing through your hands except by some remote chance, you should still be familiar with the work of these more important artists. This will provide you with a yardstick by which to judge the quality of the products of their relatively less illustrious but, even so, skilled and gifted contemporaries.

During the whole of this preparatory period you will, of course, also be going to auctions, but in the role of observer rather than of participant. You will still not, as yet, be there to buy. 'Watch and absorb' is the key phrase for this precursory stage. You are laying down a store of exact knowledge and general background impressions of the art scene as it operates in practice. You should, however, also be looking ahead to the time when you are going to become a fully fledged participant, and in consequence preparing your strategies.

This is where the consideration of your reference library needs to come in, for it has to be planned as a travelling library that can easily be loaded into the back of your car. You are going to need to have direct access to your box of books whenever you are away from home. If you are to become an effective participant in auctions, then your library is going to be a tool essential to your whole mode of operation. From this stage onwards, you are going to find yourself spending increasing amounts of time just sitting in your car and comparing the descriptions in auctioneers' catalogues with the information available from the books.

As soon as you have received your copy of an auctioneer's

catalogue through the post, then start to work through it systematically, picking on those items where you feel you already have some notion of what you might be prepared to pay. Mark in these provisional limits in pencil or ball-point pen, then go to the reference books, seeing, in particular, whether you can find any comparable prices that have been paid recently. Also mark in any previously recorded prices that might be useful to you. Having prepared the ground in this way, when you attend the auction itself, use a different colour to mark in the prices actually fetched. You can then settle down at your leisure to make the necessary comparisons.

In this way, you will gradually build up a measure of confidence in your own judgement and predictions. To begin with, you may expect to make certain forecasts that are over- or under-estimated to quite a wide extent. Do not be discouraged. Where this happens, you must try to analyse and understand the reasons why the pictures fetched the prices they did.

THE INTERNATIONAL MONEY MARKET

Perhaps you will now start to say, well, all of this is beginning to sound a fairly complicated sort of business. For our part, we have to say, if only it were that simple. There is one further factor, so far unmentioned, that you are going to need to take into account, and that is the state of the international money market. This is not a matter to which you can turn a blind eye. Its effect is to give rise to sliding scales in art prices, which means, in turn, since these slide down as well as up, that there can be no such thing as a constant, fixed price. Because a picture by the painter Jones happened to fetch £500 at an auction this time last year, it does not follow that a picture of the same size by the same artist will fetch the same sum or thereabouts at an auction today. The international money market may have altered in the meantime. Hence the money market is something that needs constant watching.

The guiding rule is that it is the relative weakness or strength of the dollar against the pound that is the governing factor. When the dollar is weak, then the market is weak, and art prices can be expected to dip downwards in response. When the dollar is strong, then the market grows to be more buoyant and the prices commanded for works of art will rise.

The economics of all this are really quite easy to understand, and logical in their own terms. In a time of a strong dollar and a weak pound, then buyers will travel from the United States to buy since their dollars are then going to obtain for them a greater number of works of art and so make their trip worthwhile. With a weak dollar and a strong pound, on the other hand, they will prefer to stay at home and concentrate on the domestic American market. Similarly, continental buyers, from France, Germany and Italy among other countries, will tend to come to Britain to buy when the pound is weak, but will find it harder to call their journeys really necessary when they have to contend with a strong pound.

Art prices may therefore be seen, in one sense, as barometric indicators of the state of the international monetary climate. It is simply because this directly affects the turnover of prices at every local auction-room the length and breadth of the country that it cannot be ignored. You cannot therefore afford to be anything except fully informed on the up-to-the-minute value of the pound *versus* the dollar. Even so, this is not something that can or should be followed blindly. Each rise or fall in the art market gathers its own momentum so that each swing will tend to go above or below the swings in the money market. It is something you will always need to bear in mind in your own calculations.

The other cause of shifts and about-turns in art values that you need to consider has what may be considered a far more arbitrary and less definable basis. It has to do with changing fashion, with the rise and fall of reputations and the types of picture that are currently being sought after or else given the cold shoulder. At any one time, there are artists who happen to be in vogue and other artists who happen to be out of favour. There is nobody who can tell you what the next change coming just around the corner is likely to be. Nobody can know what it will be until it happens.

FADS AND FASHIONS

This is a situation for which you can only hope to develop the intangible feel and flair that comes under the general heading of intuition. Certain people are more adept at it than others. Nevertheless, you can always keep a look-out for those straws in the wind that betoken a change in the making. When, for example, you suddenly notice a flurry of bidding among several dealers for an item which you would not have expected them to show much concern over, then it is quite likely that a new vogue has broken surface. If, conversely, the bidding seems to have grown unexpectedly sluggish or even to be non-existent for a painting by an artist who has previously commanded good prices, then this may be taken as an indication that the painter in question

41

has, for some reason or other, begun to drop from favour.

It would be a mistake, however, to make too heavy a meal out of this aspect. For one thing, fashions do not usually change all that quickly. For another, these are generally side-issues rather than questions of central importance. They are simply matters that you will need to take into account every now and again, and are all of a piece with the continuing processes of reassessment.

FILING SYSTEMS

A problem we all run into from time to time, unless we are exceptionally gifted with a retentive memory, is thinking at the time when we run across certain facts and details that we are going to be able to remember them. Inevitably we then discover, a short while later, that they have irretrievably faded from recall.

One way round this is to devise a memory aid in the form of a card index. It is the type of record that you can start compiling from the very first time you attend an auction. On each card you should enter data on each picture that you have singled out as holding a special interest for you. Then, where you have pitched your wits against the trends in bidding and tested these out against your ideas on a costing system, you can make a comprehensive and easily accessible record of how well you have done.

You will probably want to devise your own layout for an index card, in line with your personal interests and prefer-ences, and the example illustrated here is only a suggestion. To be useful, however, a card should obviously contain such basic information as the location and date of the auction sale, the name of the artist, the title of the picture and the medium in which it has been executed, its dimension (width x height), the price you predicted for it and the price it actually fetched. If there happen to be any obvious signs of a picture needing to be cleaned, repaired or restored, then these details should also be noted.

The most obvious approach to constructing a filing system will be to organize cards into alphabetical order according to the names of artists. This is the method that will give you the most immediate access to the information the cards contain whenever you want to check or make a comparison. It is this system that will constitute your *reference* index. When you come to buy and sell, you will, of course, find you need to make a second index so that you have a properly filed record of all the pictures that have actually passed through your hands.

Given the recent developments in word processors and

personal computers, and the general lowering of prices that
has put some excellent sets of equipment within reach of a
wide public, you may come to consider it worth your while
to invest in an electronic storage system. You will need to
shop around carefully to see which type of computer is going
to best suit your purpose and your pocket, but most systems
these days have card-index options where you can design the
layout for your own template. Once you have mastered the
working of a system, then the recording, storage and retrieval
of all information can become continual on a fast and highly
efficient basis. (But it should never entirely supplant your
conventional card-index systems since computer discs can
be vulnerable to mistakes in operation, and especially to
damage by dust, and the idea of losing data painstakingly
accumulated over the course of a long period through a simple mishap when you have not perhaps kept your back-up
discs up to date is a prospect not to be contemplated.)

The final source of record that you should, of course,
maintain is an address-book with the addresses of all your
contacts and clients, incorporating all relevant annotations
about their interests, specialities and wants. This, too,
is the kind of information that can be usefully stored
on a computer.

DATE OF AUCTION	ARTIST	SUBJECT	MEDIUM	SIZE (width + depth)	CONDITION	PRICE
3/3/1988 Biddlens & Boy	Frank Dauber	River & Punt	Oil on canvas	12 x 10	Fair (minor flaking)	£120 -

A simple index-card system. (The headings can be hand-written.)

SOCIAL
GRACES

One of the main assets you can cultivate in yourself is in adopting a general affableness and ease of manner towards everybody you meet. As you go to more and more auctions, so you will find you come to recognize increasing numbers of faces. It will do you no harm to introduce yourself to them and cultivate them in a pleasant way. In fact you may be sure that affability is an attribute that will, in the long run, do you a service in return. *Remember always, that everyone who attends an auction is a potential customer, not a potential rival.* In due course, you are likely to find that your new acquaintances start to offer you their cards and tell you how they are watching out at the moment for, it might be, pictures of horses, and if you should come across any, to get in touch.

At this point you may ask, well, so what about these stories we have all heard concerning dealers' price rings and price fixings, not to mention the impossibility of outsiders being able to enter into competition where these charmed circles are operating? The myth of the price ring certainly dies hard, but you will soon find out from your personal dealings in the arena that it is nothing you need to entertain any fears over. So long as you go to the right drinking-places, get your face known and seen on appropriate occasions and avoid being opinionated on subjects about which you as yet know very little, then this will all turn out to be a sufficient *entrée*.

There is, of course, also the matter of the design and printing of your own card to be considered. Like the styles adopted in making bids, this can involve various questions of personal taste. By all means have an elaborate card designed with fancy typography if that is what you desire. There is much to be said, however, for the simplest possible style, consisting, perhaps, of no more than your name in plain, elegant lettering. Such a card will make its mark far more directly and memorably than a card that is cluttered with information. If you should also be asked for your address and telephone number, then this can be added on a printed sticker such as you can order from any professional stationers. You may still be within the bounds of your initial period of six months or so of groundwork, but getting your card printed should nevertheless be one of your first priorities.

Even though the time for you to enter into the bidding may not as yet have come round, you should still get into the way of offering the auctioneer your card and stating your interest in doing some bidding at a point in the near future. This is all, once again, a part of the process of putting yourself into circulation and getting yourself known.

A little later on, when you do come to bid with serious intent, you will need to be able to present your card together with bankers' references, if these are required. But now, just for the moment, the time has come when you should set aside periods when you can turn your back on the gregarious auction-room scene and knuckle down to a few sessions of serious, solitary study.

BACK TO THE READING ROOMS

In whatever county or district you happen to live, you should now make it your business to find out which one of your city or county reference libraries houses the main, most comprehensive collection of art books for your area. As soon as you know where to go, plan to spend as much time there as you can possibly spare, studying and reading in what will hopefully be a quiet and cloistered atmosphere. Read through every text you can find on aspects of English art from the nineteenth through to the early twentieth century. Read up all you can on English water-colours and oils, English landscapes and seascapes, English *genre* paintings.

We are not, in this instance, concerned with the books you need to acquire for your personal reference collection, but with the books that will help you to build up your store of background knowledge. They may be monographs on individual artists, or they may be studies of groups or schools or periods of painting. The object of the exercise is for you to soak up every piece of information on which you can lay hands, in terms both of the printed texts and of the examples of paintings given in the illustrations. You should literally saturate yourself in the subject so that, in the future, the name of an artist in a catalogue or the look and style of a particular painting will strike a familiar chord and thus enable you to make a connection and spot an association. What you are doing, in fact, is constructing an informed context within which you will be able to function.

ESSENTIAL SUBSCRIPTIONS

One of the best initial investments you can make will be to take out a subscription to the organization known as the Antique Collectors' Club. The current annual subscription (1988) is £15.95 for UK members, but these things are unfortunately not constant. You would therefore be advised to write, in the first instance, to the Antique Collectors' Club, 5 Church Street, Woodbridge, Suffolk IP12 1DS, and ask them to forward you an application form for membership.

The club has been running since 1966, and although

it operates from what may sound like a quiet provincial backwater of East Anglia in the United Kingdom, it has established itself over the course of more than two decades until, today, it can boast of an extensive international membership. It took as its motto, 'For collectors — by collectors — about collecting', so implying that its pitch is not intended to be towards the professionals, but much rather in the direction of keeping amateur collectors in touch with latest trends and prices being paid; and to provide them with the means to make contact with like-minded enthusiasts in their own localities, in different parts of the country and abroad. To serve this end, they have founded the journal, *Antique Collecting* (eleven issues a year).

Once you have paid your annual subscription, the Antique Collectors' Club will send you each issue of *Antique Collecting* on publication. As you will soon discover, this constitutes an invaluable, well-informed guide to all aspects of collecting, including pictures and prints of every kind, each issue containing articles that are both authoritative and interesting to read. The journal is internationally respected for its range, standards and independence of viewpoint.

The writers who contribute to the magazine are recruited from among the ranks of collectors, experts and enthusiasts, dealers and auctioneers. They include, in other words, people who are fully aware of the latest trends in their areas of specialization. The articles themselves incorporate specific comments on price tendencies and whatever areas are being freshly explored by collectors, and hence which are the ones most likely to represent an investment potential. They also set out to give, among other themes, more general background accounts of the lives of individual artists or the histories of schools of art.

One of the most positive features of the magazine is its generosity of illustration, both in the articles and in the many advertisements it carries, inserted by dealers and galleries. These are certainly useful for anyone currently engaged in developing an eye for good workmanship in any area of the arts and crafts. A secondary virtue with regard to the illustrations is the fact that there is a declared editorial policy to avoid depicting rare museum pieces, but instead to concentrate on the type of material that turns up in antique shops, galleries and auctions — the sort of stuff, in other words, that the amateur and part-time collector is going to come across in the normal course of events.

As with your studies of the art books in libraries, you should seize the chance being offered you here to soak up the pictures, visually speaking, as well as the texts of the articles themselves. Where it seems useful to do so, you should note in your card index of background information any records that relate to your sphere of interest.

You will also find that *Antique Collecting* contains current lists of regional collectors' clubs and their activities, as well as — most vital from your point of view — an auction calendar compiled on a countrywide basis. This represents, in fact, your single most important source of information on the auctions that are held regularly throughout the United Kingdom. Out of it you can select and fashion your personal calendar of those auctions that are of particular interest to your own range of interests.

The 'For Sale' and 'Wanted' columns will themselves repay close attention and study, offering, as they do, food for thought on, and many concrete indicators of, the items at present being sought after by dealers and collectors up and down the country. These columns also contain many examples of the prices being asked as well as those being offered, and so they will assist you in any efforts to build up a general context for your ideas on what to pay and what to ask or aim for when it comes to selling an item on to a dealer. What is more, you could, from time to time, find the columns useful for making either a purchase or a sale.

Another function of the club is to publish, under its own imprint, books for collectors. A catalogue of these is available, and the titles listed are highly recommended for their reliability and comprehensiveness. Among them are several of the volumes that you will need to acquire for your own reference library (for the complete suggested list, see below). As a club member, you may find that you are eligible to buy certain books at special pre-publication prices.

Subscribing to the Antique Collectors' Club is clearly going to bring you many benefits, including access to a whole range of consequential and incidental information in the highways and byways of dealing and collecting. Apart from anything else, you will find yourself provided with a rapid route to familiarity both with your essential sources of information and the networks of auction houses, dealers and galleries as these are spread and scattered throughout the United Kingdom. The subscription will, in other words, be excellent value.

A further subscription that you will find brings invaluable returns will be one to the *Antiques Trade Gazette*, a weekly trade paper published from 17 Whitcomb Street, London WC2H 7PL. This is packed with up-to-date news of the trade in general, contains many advertisements of sales, fairs and markets, and, important for our purposes, interesting records of current prices fetched by individual pictures.

As soon as you know who those auctioneers are on whom you are going to be calling regularly, then, as we have said already, it will be sensible to take out a year's subscription to each of their catalogue mailing lists. This will represent another modest outlay, but it, too, will have its value confirmed. In fact you will probably only have to pay a subscription for the first year, since in future years, once you are known, you will automatically be on the mailing lists and so will receive catalogues as a recognized client.

QUESTIONS OF TERRITORY

As you come to compile your calendar of auctions, you will need to bear in mind that, while certain reasons exist as to why you should sometimes attend the prestigious sales held at Sotheby's and Christie's, bidding and buying is certainly not among them. Your *raison d'être* for attending these sales would mainly be to observe and see what goes on. There is no point in your going to buy from these particular sources of supply, since you will then be doing so in competition with some of the country's leading galleries and dealers. To put it another way, you will be competing against your own buyers.

Apart from that, the work on sale will generally be of a higher quality than you will want to be concerning yourself with at the present time. It will also remain largely outside your price bracket. Therefore you should resign yourself to the fact that this is not your territory. You ought instead to be setting your sights on the auctions taking place all the time in the less centrally placed locations of market towns and provincial communities.

The fact of the matter is that provincial auctions are not, broadly speaking, especially accessible to the big dealers who operate within the commercial centres. Even if they were inclined to try to cover them all, the actual number of events would make this a physical impossibility and take them away from their own showrooms, where they do their real business, for far too long. Of course, if they do happen to have wind of something very out of the ordinary coming on to the market, they are likely to make it their business to be there, or, at least, to be represented. But this is only likely to happen with relative rarity. Any item known beforehand to carry an especially high interest value will most probably have been referred direct to the valuers at Sotheby's or Christie's in the first place. Anything disposable to the big dealers is anyway going to find its way into their hands through the agency of the middle men who make up the dealers' chains. The high-flying dealers do not, on the whole, need to keep travelling far and wide to gather in their wares.

The point for you in all of this is that you are likely to find that, as you come to be better known in the field — and as others come to regard you as a reliable individual who does his homework — larger dealers will begin to ask you to bid on their behalf. The usual basis for this service is a mutually agreed commission on the price paid to secure. It is also possible, once you are known and have extended your overall range of contacts, that you could be approached by foreign clients to undertake the same kind of service. These are not eventualities you can count on, but possibilities to be borne in mind for the future. Whether or not they come to pass will depend entirely on your own ability to build up a reputation for reliability and soundness of judgement.

It is a good idea, as you compile your calendar of auctions, to work out a tour of, say, six auctions that you plan to attend regularly. If your time allows it, aim to attend an average of one auction a week. Your calendar will, as a matter of course, include all those auctions that fall broadly within your geographical area, but the further you can move out from London in planning your circuit, the better the prospects will be. Once you have marked down your auctions, make it your business to become known to the auctioneers and to all the others who attend them. Become, in other words, a known face. Give yourself the odd day or two away from home, book in at a pleasant hotel and in general set out to enjoy yourself.

At no point should you cease soaking up the atmosphere and watching the details of bidding and other people's idiosyncracies of gesture. Begin to give the development of your own auction manner some attention. Your style does not need to be flamboyant, eccentric or showy. In fact a more subdued style may be preferable, not unlike the style of the practised poker player. That is not to say that you should, in the effort of trying to avoid giving away how keen you are, actually appear to be unkeen. It is simply important to cultivate a certain nonchalance in your manner of approach.

We have already emphasized how important it is for you to make a point of arriving for each auction's viewing day in plenty of time so that you do not have to rush through anything at any stage. Apart from any other aspects involved, you need to remember that it is wise to allow for a margin of time simply to sit in your car and check on the names of artists together with other details and the price indexes contained in the collection of essential reference volumes that you have with you in the back of your vehicle.

REFERENCE BOOKS

To round off this chapter on your essential sources of information, it only remains to list those books that are going to be indispensable to you — the ones that are going to make up your own mobile reference library and will travel with you every time you attend an auction. Together with your card indexes, these will represent your personal department of essential information — your reservoir of vital facts.

Prices of books vary and change with time, and people tend to complain that they seem to be growing more expensive. The prices we list were correct at the time of going to press, but they may, of course, have been revised subsequently. At the current rates, however, you will need to set aside something in the region of £250 to finance the business of putting together a basic collection. Books are therefore likely to be your single most noticeable outlay in the first instance. Some of them are, moreover, annual publications where you will need to purchase the new edition each year if you are to keep yourself in touch with the most up-to-date information.

New books on art and on various aspects of collecting are, of course, continually being published. As you become more familiar with the literature, you will doubtless come across other books that you will recognize as being useful to your specific requirements and decide to purchase them in due course. The titles given in the list that follows are the basis — the nucleus, if you like — of your collection. They are the ones you simply cannot afford to be without whenever and wherever you are doing business.

The Annual Arts Sales Index, 2 volumes, edited by Richard Hislop. Art Sales Index Ltd., £56.00. As an annual publication, this is the most expensive individual item you are going to have to buy. Its value, however, is self-evident. It provides a comprehensive record of the prices fetched for every work of art sold at auction in the United Kingdom during the course of the previous year.

The Lyle Official Arts Review compiled by Tony Curtis. Lyle Publications, £12.95. With over 2,000 illustrations and its information garnered from all leading European and North American auction houses, this annual publication records prices (sterling equivalents next to prices in other currencies), as well as much other useful data for pictures sold over the course of a year.

The Guide to the Antique Shops of Britain, Antique Collectors' Club, £8.95. Here is another publication that is updated annually. Published in July each year, it contains many details of information on galleries, who their proprietors are, what their preferences are for types of stock, the price ranges they aim for, even where to find parking if you call to visit them. An incidental benefit of this title is that it can save you a wasted journey where a gallery has moved or gone out of business.

The Dictionary of British Artists, 1880-1940 compiled by J. Johnson and A. Greutzner. Antique Collectors' Club, £35. The entries in this dictionary contain concise biographical notes on more than 40,000 artists.

The Dictionary of British Watercolour Artists up to 1920 by H.L. Mallalieu. 2 volumes, vol. I: text; vol. II: plates. Antique Collectors' Club, £22.50 each volume. A standard work, illustrated with 795 plates, whose text contains comments on the style of as well as biographical information for almost 3,500 artists.

A Dictionary of British Artists Working 1900-1950 by Grant M. Waters. 2 volumes, Eastbourne Fine Art, £16.50. A useful book for tracking down lesser-known artists of the present century.

The Dictionary of Victorian Painters, second edition, by Christopher Wood. Antique Collectors' Club, £35. Another standard work, covering approximately 11,000 artists of the Victorian era.

A Dictionary of Artists Who Exhibited Works in the Principal London Exhibitions from 1760-1893 by Algernon Graves. Kingsmead Reprints, £22.50. Compiled from original sources, this compendium from the Georgian to the Victorian period is indispensable.

Armed with these books when you go to an auction's viewing day, you can slip away on one side for a few moments to mark down in the auctioneer's catalogue those pictures in which you have a *potential* interest, annotating the catalogue's margins with the prices you anticipate you might have to pay to secure them.

Remember that you will in the earlier days be looking not for large expensive oil-paintings, but for smaller oils

Two examples of *staffage*: (Above) *The Young Harvesters, Whitchurch, Near Bristol* by W. Muller. Oil on canvas. 1843. (Right) *Figure in Landscape* by Charles Burleigh (d. 1956). Oil on canvas. Early twentieth century.

along with water-colours or drawings — for the *signed* works of minor artists. The authenticity of each picture — the question of its provenance — is an important matter for the galleries you will be selling to. At the outset, you will be well advised to stick with those categories of subject that are known to be the most popular:

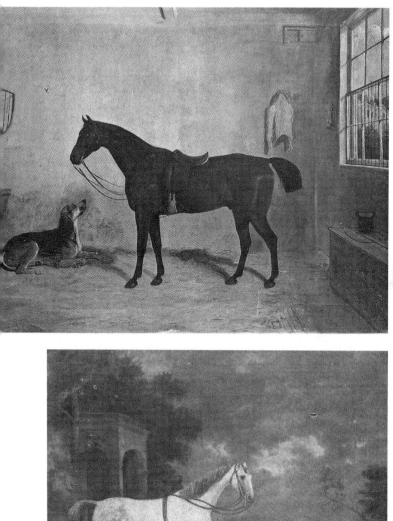

An equestrian portrait: *A Saddled Dark Bay Hunter with a Hound in a Stable* by Edward Walter Webb. Mid nineteenth-century.

A Dappled Grey Hunter with a Dog in a Landscape by Francis Sartorius (1734-1804). Oil on canvas.

1. Landscapes with *staffage* — that is to say, landscapes that contain a figure or figures to offset the landscape itself.

2. Animal subjects, especially horses, with or without riders. Dogs, cats, fluffy kittens, and animals with big, appealing eyes then follow in order of popularity.

A Farmer with a Harnessed Horse in a stable by Thomas Weaver (1775-1843). Oil on canvas.

Bulldogs and a Hound Outside a Kennel by John Frederick Herring, Snr. (1795-1865)

Still-life of Fruit by
Joseph Rhodes
(1782-1854). Oil on
canvas. 1833.

*Fairies Riding on a
Dragon* (from *A
Book Full of
Nonsense*) by
Richard Doyle
(1824-83).

3. Still-lives.

4. Fairy pictures.

Portraits of a Gentleman and his Wife by Arthur Devis (c.1711-1787). A pair, both oil on panel.

Portraits of children and animals always find a market. *Portrait of a Young Girl with Her Pet Spaniel* by Tilly Kettle (1735-86). Oil on canvas, unframed.

5. *Genre* pictures, showing people going about their daily concerns. The later the period to which these belong, the less

View of Shipping at Seville by Lionel Edwards (1878-1966) Oil on canvas.

An Impressionist marine painting by P. Hodds, a British artist.

overtly moral they are likely to be; but the more picturesque they are, the easier they will be to dispose of.

6. Pairs of portraits. Matching pairs are liked by the galleries, and especially by interior decorators. The portraits should, however, invariably be of good-looking people. (It has to be admitted that what is generally asked of them is that they be not so much art as effective decoration.)

7. Marine paintings. The bay of Naples is a particular favourite.

The Brig Betty in Two Positions off a Harbour Mouth by H. Collins. Oil on canvas. Signed and dated 1810.

Finally, for a statement that cannot be made too often. At an auction, so long as the prices seem to be right, you should always go for work that has a strong appeal to you personally. If, by any chance, you then fail to sell a picture at a profit, you will at least be able to enjoy living with it for a year or two, until the time comes round when you can dispose of it. At the very least, so long as you have bought with reasonable care, you should be able to put it in an auction and so get your money back. The likelihood is, however, that you will be able to sell it and show the sort of margin of profit for which you have been waiting.

The history of painting itself need concern us only briefly here. Various excellent books on the subject are available, and you are sure to come across some of them in the course of your background reading. Suffice it to say that the activities we term artistic go far back into the prehistory of mankind.

The famous prehistoric Stone Age paintings on the walls of the caves at Lascaux in the Dordogne region of France, which experts have dated back to about 20,000 B.C., were most probably done for religious or magical reasons rather than out of anything we would today call 'artistic inspiration' or 'aesthetic impulse'. The animals that the cave murals depict with such vividness and grace are, we can only speculate, intended to be the tribal totems and illustrate sources of sustenance for a hunting people. Depicting the animals may have been thought to have assisted in the hunting of them through rituals of sympathetic magic; or even to propitiate the spirits of the creatures whose killing was necessary for the tribe to survive.

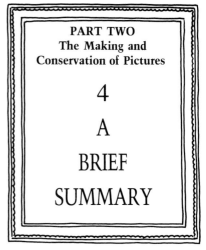

PART TWO
The Making and
Conservation of Pictures

4

A

BRIEF

SUMMARY

The Stone Age cave painters, working with their limited palette, performed wonders. Their pigments, based on powdered earths and only a few minerals, gave mainly a range of yellows, reds and dark browns. At a later stage of artistic development, the Ancient Egyptian tomb painters, who were working for the Pharaohs from about the time of the 6th Dynasty (late in the third millennium B.C.), had some striking blues available in the form of azurite (a copper carbonate) and other copper-based compounds.

In this way, with each new tradition in painting, the palette went on steadily developing in terms of range and versatility. First during Roman times, and then in the Middle Ages, many other substances, including waxes of various types as well as vegetable dyes and colours of animal origin, came to be added to the repertoire of pigments. Subsequently, the artist's palette has never, throughout recorded history, ceased to expand, both in the range of colour tones obtainable and in the technical methods and types of material used in their manufacture.

So far as the subjects of paintings are concerned, the vision and special talent of artists continued, for many centuries, to be harnessed to the causes of religion, the state or private patronage. This continued to be so right down to what are very recent times indeed within the overall span of human history. The notion of the artist as being someone who arrives at an individuality of expression out of his or her internal life, then works autonomously, would never really have occurred to anyone before the end of the eighteenth century. It was only in Enlightenment times that romanticism in art brought into existence the image of the artist as a being whose function is to probe, challenge and question the assumptions of the *status quo*. Nevertheless, one of the signs of a good or great artist has always been the ability to test a skill against the boundaries and limitations imposed by the materials he uses and the society he inhabits.

The most important technique to be evolved in the earlier stages of the history of portable painting was that of *tempera*. Broadly speaking, the word means the use of paints that are water soluble, the pigments being held in an emulsion that can either be diluted further or alternatively thickened up in line with whatever colour values are being sought. In its most specific meaning, tempera refers to *egg tempera* technique, where the binding agent used for the pigments was the yolk of an egg, carefully extracted from its sac. This gave the paints, once they had dried, a uniquely satiny and much-admired quality of finish.

Variations in tempera technique were used, during the Middle Ages, for such varied purposes as painting on wooden panels, creating murals or *secco* frescoes (on dry as opposed to wet plaster) on church walls, or the illumination of manuscripts. Tempera had, at its best, a durability that was both remarkable and reliable. Egg tempera showed itself to possess an elasticity that effectively prevented it shrinking or cracking. Moreover, the colours, once they had set, remained new and fresh in appearance. On the other hand, tempera did have a number of quite basic disadvantages. For one thing, an artist never quite knew how the colours were going to turn out until they had actually dried; for another, the medium was subject to a hazardous vulnerability to damp and mould where works were kept in less than ideal conditions. Notwithstanding its drawbacks, however, tempera held its position as the most generally used artistic medium all the way through to the end of the Middle Ages. It has even, during the twentieth century, surfaced in new guises.

So far as we are concerned, the medieval artist as often as not remains an anonymous figure who fulfilled his vocation by decorating the interiors of cathedrals and churches as well as the houses of the aristocracy or the homes of wealthy merchants. It is only very rarely that the trace of a name has been passed down, and where an artist's name is identifiable, this is most likely to be through some accident of survival in the historical records. It is only as time progresses that the names of individual artists begin to emerge more regularly, and with the names a sense of there being a certain individual personality or genius behind a definable body of work.

Initially, there developed out of these circumstances the tradition of the artist as a kind of superior artisan. He had his studio and employed his apprentices and he painted to fulfil commissions for the rich and powerful; he worked, in other words, to enhance the status in society of those who happened to be his patrons. At the very apex of the Renaissance, this remained much the social position of even Michelangelo, Leonardo and Raphael in relation to those who provided them with their livelihoods, however much we, today, may see these artists as having been giants in the intellectual history of mankind.

As the individual identities of artists and schools of art came to be more strongly recognizable, however, so did portraiture move forward to take its place as a distinct and separate strand in artistic tradition. The portrait as such was something that had always existed in certain contexts. The heads of monarchs, for example, have been reproduced on coins since time immemorial. There were also the ideal-ized depictions of the Pharaohs in their tombs, and then the highly realistic paintings on wooden coffin lids from the later Romano-Egyptian period, to take up some early examples. In Ancient Rome itself, the stone portrait bust attained a high level of realism, so that when we see specimens of these in museums today, we do not find it hard to think of them as being of men or women whom we would recognize if we saw them in the street.

The figures carved in wood or stone in medieval churches may often incorporate likenesses of local personalities, in the same way that the faces in stained-glass windows may sometimes be portraits. But the idea of the 'portrait' as a portable artefact in its own right — one that records a person or groups of people for posterity — only begins to emerge strongly during the Renaissance period. This corresponds with the time from early in the fifteenth century when the technique of oil-painting begins to move into the forefront and starts to displace the supremacy of tempera as the preferred artistic medium.

The Renaissance is the term used to describe the period in the history of art that began in Italy in about 1420 and moved towards fresh definitions of classical ideas combined with a humanistic view of mankind's universal destiny and dignity. It marked an emergence from the society of the late Middle Ages, and achieved its peak during only one extraordinary quarter of a century, from about 1500 to 1527 — the period known as the High Renaissance. It was this that provided the fertile soil that fostered and allowed the fulfilment of genius in the cases of three of the greatest artists of all time, Leonardo da Vinci, Raphael and Michelangelo. Whether these men made the Renaissance, or whether the Renaissance made them, could seem to be getting into an argument corresponding to whether the egg came before the chicken or vice versa. Had it lacked their presence, the Renaissance could surely never have had the momentum of influence that it did possess, whose ripples may still be traced down to the present time.

While the Renaissance is therefore a cornerstone to any study of the history of art, it is also immeasurably important in the development of Western thought and the rationalism that makes up its central thread. Its secular emphasis on the importance of the individual may be seen as having fathered consequences that re-emerged in all sorts of ways during the following centuries, in the fields of philosophy, religion and politics, science and technology, as much as they did in art. From one viewpoint, it might be thought that the history of art has been a regression, a steady downhill process as time carries us ever further from the dazzling zenith the movement had reached by the 1520s. An alternative viewpoint might see the liberation of spirit and imagination made possible by the Renaissance as being directly responsible for the infinite variety and explorativeness shown by the schools and movements of Western art during the succeeding four centuries.

One of the main effects of an increasing sense of individualism among artists was the growth of conscious movements in art, such as the great Romantic Movement of the early nineteenth century, or, a little later on, the British Pre-Raphaelite Movement. Side by side with this there went an increasing preoccupation with how the artist views the world and interprets it in terms of images abstracted from the totality of his sense of vision. Thus, as we move into the modern era, we find the movements, schools and 'isms' of painting proliferating and splitting away, and even at times, like political parties, producing their own manifestos. Their history has also been one of tending to outrage the public, especially at the point of their first impact. This was the case with Impressionism, which was especially concerned with the way light struck the retina of the eye, and then with the other modern movements such as Expressionism (the expression of inner states of being though the painted object), Cubism (the underlying geometric structures of objects), Surrealism (the direct expression of the unconscious through dream images), or Abstractionism (the use of paint in a way that moves away from the representational altogether). Therefore, while we may sometimes see the art of our own civilization as having been highly uneven in control and quality, perhaps never again quite hitting the original peak of vision and greatness of the Renaissance, it has gathered an impressive richness. Still, today, the ripples continue to spread ever wider and to reach after the possibilities offered by new technologies.

Thus do innovations in art continue to develop hand in hand with technical advances, while those who collect and enjoy art need to maintain at least a basic background knowledge of how pictures of every kind come into being. Our main focus in this section is therefore on the actual manufacturing of pictures and the many ways in which these have been made, principally over the past two hundred years or so. In the next three chapters, we turn to giving concise descriptions of artists' methods of working, dealing with these under the headings of the three main divisions of art: paintings, drawings and prints.

5
PAINTINGS

OIL-
PAINTING

A whole miscellany of oils, of animal, vegetable and mineral origin, have been used in painting, with variable success, since earliest times. Out of several centuries of trial and error, the true ancestors of oil-painting, as we understand it today, eventually came into existence, probably some time during the early fifteenth century. It was Vasari, the Italian author of *Lives of the Most Excellent Painters, Sculptors and Architects* (1550), who claimed the inventor of oil-painting to be the Flemish artist, Jan van Eyck, who died c. 1441. It is a claim that has been popularly accepted, but one that has also been much argued over by scholars. Van Eyck's role could well have been similar to that of so many so-called inventors in advances made in any technological field: that of being the one who selected, coordinated and adapted out of the best options available among the whole range of ideas that happened to be around at the time they were active. There were certainly other painters who were simultaneously working along the same lines as Van Eyck.

Whatever the true facts of its origins, oil-painting soon established itself as a medium fully capable of overcoming some of the disadvantages of tempera, though at the outset the underpainting was often still done in tempera with the oil on top. With oil-painting the artist knew, for a start, that the colours in the oils on his palette would correspond with the colours as these appeared in the finished painting. An additional advantage came with the fact that it was possible to use a far wider variety of materials as backing. Pictures were soon being painted not only on wooden board, copper sheeting, ceramics and glass, but also, and most importantly, on textile in the form of linen canvas.

Oil-painting in the classic sense — the type of easel painting on a canvas that was to form the backbone of the *ouevres* of all the great masters during the succeeding centuries — evolved out of the realization that, if you are going to paint on it, then your piece of canvas first needs to be stretched and secured across a frame. It needs to be stretched tightly, but not as tightly as the skin of a drum, for instance. This means, in turn, that the tension in a canvas has to be adjustable if the painting is to remain in a good state of preservation. Without this ability to adjust, such atmospheric factors as temperature and humidity are going to have an effect and take their toll as they cause the canvas to expand or contract. The chances of survival of an oil-painting on canvas are going to be considerably reduced if it should start to buckle or slacken until the point where the paint begins to crack or flake or worse.

The wooden frame on which a canvas is stretched is termed the *stretcher*, and on to this the canvas is fastened, its weave (the warp and the woof) carefully squared off with the battens. The fastening of the canvas to the sides of the stretcher should then be done with copper tacks, since these will not, like those made out of iron or steel, corrode and start eating into the material. Wedges, which are tapped gently into the mitred slots in each of the stretcher's corners — one successive tap at a time for each wedge — thereafter adjust the tension until it is at a pitch that may be judged to be appropriate.

In this way the painter is provided with his *canvas*, but before he can paint on it he needs to coat it with a recommended type of size to protect the material itself. Once the size has dried, he then has to prime the canvas (usually applying two coats of primer) to complete the initial preparation for the surface on which he will actually be able to create his picture. The type of canvas used, its weave, the structure of the frame used in making the stretcher and the kind of tacks that go to complete the fastening can all provide guide-lines for confirming the date or period for a particular work of art — always provided, of course, that it has not been remounted on new canvas during the course of a rescue operation or drastic restoration.

The traditional oil-painting has often been likened to a kind of sandwich. It is, in fact, made up from a sequence of layers, the sized and primed canvas forming the base. The actual painting process begins with the application of the *imprimatura*, a thin coating of oil colour diluted with turpentine to take the edge off the stark whiteness of the primed canvas and to give the painting its dominant tone. Once this is in place, the painting itself can begin in earnest.

It is said that the great Venetian painter Titian (c. 1490-1576) made a statement to the effect that a painter who knows his business needs no more than three colours in his palette. The earlier masters in oils in fact probably used only about half a dozen at any one time. They acquired their pigments in a raw state, and then set their apprentices to work to grind them up and mix them with their preferred oil base — most commonly linseed. The steady advances in technology from Renaissance times onward did not neglect the needs of painters, and in due course various fresh pigments were added to extend the potential colour repertoire. The period following on from the later eighteenth century, which corresponded with the founding period of the Industrial Revolution, also saw the synthesizing of many pigments alongside other developments that were actually side-products of industrial processes.

By the middle of the nineteenth century, it had ceased to be necessary for an artist to buy his paints in a raw state and prepare them in his studio. He could, instead, obtain them direct from an artist's supplier, and buy them most conveniently moreover in the recently developed flexible tin tubes designed with screw tops to prevent the paints drying out while they were in storage or use.

It is not usually realized how the invention of the paint tube imposed what could be claimed as the greatest revolution in oil-painting following its inception. For one thing, it meant that the oil-painter could set foot outside the studio and go out and about with equipment and paints, so creating pictures direct from nature. For another, the fluid working qualities of the new paints were curiously different from those obtained when using the old methods. A certain capability for creating flow was lost, making it necessary to adopt changes in painting technique. These involved painting with hog's hair or sable brushes that had blunter, more stubby ends than those used by the previous generation of artists.

The process of new pigments coming on to the market has continued down to the present time. (Artists' manufacturers today often present a bewildering array of alternatives in their catalogues, though it remains open to debate whether the wideness of choice necessarily adds to the quality or durability of the finished product.) A tendency to experiment or pursue a particular habit or notion can lead, as time goes on, to formidable challenges for picture conservators and restorers. These professionals can find themselves having to work to counteract all sorts of little tricks and conservation time-bombs that are the results of techniques or innovations that have turned out to be ill-advised.

One of the most illustrious cases in point on this score is provided by Sir Joshua Reynolds (1723-92), whose incorrigible fascination with the technicalities of painting meant that he never stopped tampering and experimenting with methods. This gave William Blake the chance to make his famous gibe against his old enemy in his annotations to his copy of Reynolds's *Discourses*:

When Sir Joshua Reynolds died
All Nature was degraded;
The King drop'd a tear into the Queen's Ear,
And all his Pictures Faded.

For fade Reynolds's paintings did indeed, the flesh-tones of the subjects in his portraits draining into bloodlessness, and all because he had used certain notoriously fugitive pigments. Even Reynolds himself once ironically lamented that his painting 'came off with flying colours'. He left posterity a very catalogue of errors and many pictures, done in the Grand Manner, whose ruin was in-built.

It was nevertheless the very versatility of oil-painting that ensured the medium would come to constitute a major

Anne, Countess of Albemarle by Sir Joshua Reynolds (1723-92). As with so many of Reynolds's portraits, the flesh tones have faded. Oil on canvas.

branch of the pictorial arts. Oils allow for a great variety of effects, from subtlety and delicacy of detail and tone to broad, bold strokes and colours. They leave the artist free to construct his picture out of succeeding layers of paint, and also able to correct misjudgements, for there is never any problem about overlaying whatever lies beneath with a fresh application of paint.

Diluted with turpentine, oil-paints may, on the one hand, be used very thinly; or they may, on the other, be applied directly in thick wadges or even worked with a painting knife instead of a brush — the effect termed *impasto*. Oils are as adaptable to small flower paintings or portraits rich in details of dress texture or decoration as they are to large-scale landscapes or seascapes; or to strongly expressive works extending all the way into the purely abstract. In other words, there is no subject under the sun that cannot be adapted to a suitable treatment in oils where an artist wishes to attempt it.

Once an oil-painting has been completed, it will be left to stand for a while. The paint needs to be allowed to go through a natural process of setting and hardening. This usually takes about six months. Afterwards, the final layer of the 'sandwich' is put in position in the form of an application of varnish, the varnish in fact serving two purposes. First, it creates a tangible protective barrier between the paint and the outer world; and secondly, it intensifies and enhances the colour tones of the paints themselves.

In a sense, therefore, an oil-painting is not truly finished until it has been given its top layer of varnish. Modern varnishes display far more consistent qualities than those that were originally used on paintings more than thirty or forty years old. The old varnishes, made from natural resins, all had varying degrees of a tendency to darken or yellow and crack in time, so leaving a legacy of conservation problems for future generations and helping to keep picture restorers in bread-and-butter work. We shall be looking at the various ways in which experts deal with these problems when we come to Chapter 8 (page 101).

While the majority of oil-painting is still carried out on canvas, a variety of other supports are used by artists, these consisting mainly of types of woodboard or hardboard. Where a wooden panel is used, it should be of well-seasoned timber, preferably mahogany, and should be cradled (that is to say, have two vertical panels screwed to the back) to prevent it warping. Plywood (preferably 8-ply) and hardboard panels also need cradling, as do thick cardboard or strawboard panels; these latter, incidentally, can make surprisingly serviceable and durable supports. Chipboard also makes a good support, and it needs no cradling, though it can become rather friable at the corners or along the edges. It is possible to glue muslin to chipboard to make a very acceptable support, and paper glued to hardboard is used in a similar way at times. Oil sketches can, in fact, be done on paper sized with gelatine. Research meanwhile continues with attempts to produce an entirely satisfactory synthetic canvas material, but this remains as yet a chancy area. While the synthetic canvases so far produced are cheap and lightweight, their behaviour over a period of time is likely to be unpredictable and it is possible they could turn brittle.

The use of water-colour holds a distinguished position which may be said to represent a continuous thread that runs through the whole of the long tradition of Chinese and Japanese art. In Western art, however, water-colour may be said to occupy a quite specific niche, and although types of water-colour are known, for instance, on Egyptian papyrus rolls, the term 'water-colour' has come to mean a particular technique distinct from gouache or tempera — these, of course, also being founded on water-based as opposed to oil-based paints.

WATER-COLOURS

In the manufacture of water-colour paints, the pigment is mixed with a water-soluble glue (most usually gum arabic), which gives it a transparent quality once it has been thinned with water. It is this very quality of transparency that the artist then exploits, using the paint mixed with water as a wash so that the light continues to shine through from the surface of the paper underneath the paint. In other words, the artist creates the lighting effects, along with much of the colour intensity, by the extent to which he allows the paper to show through. This makes it the very reverse of a gouache technique (see below), although in practice the two techniques can be, and often are, mixed in the same picture.

High-quality paper is essential when working with water-colour, for a cheap paper will rob the pigments of much of their potential life and liveliness and so represent a false economy from the point of view of any serious artist. Handmade papers, manufactured from pulped linen rags, are reckoned to be the kind most generally preferred. Papers are supplied in a wide variety of grades (graded according to weight), and vary in thickness and the relative fineness or coarseness of their grain. The grain itself is an important component in creating a lustre and sparkle in the finished effect of a picture, since the light from the dips in the grain is projected back more strongly where the paint, in effect, passes over the top of them.

Investing in cheap brushes is another economy that is not to be recommended for the water-colourist. A battery of brushes is needed, ranging from the broad — to apply background washes — to the very fine, and good brushes are expensive, the best and most costly of them being made of sable. Ox, camel or squirrel hair brushes do, however, make quite acceptable substitutes. Sponges, rags or tissues may also be utilized at times to gain special effects to augment the brush-work.

The great advance in water-colour development in fact occurred in Britain during the eighteenth and early nineteenth centuries. It has been described as the most important contribution made by England to European art history and has led to water-colour painting sometimes being referred to as 'the English Manner'. Prior to this, there had been artists who used water-colour from time to time, though the paintings they did in this medium only amounted to a small proportion of their output. As a consequence, water-colours from earlier centuries are considerable rarities. Nevertheless, there are some marvellous and famous examples, such as the landscapes and other studies of natural history (animals and grasses) that Albrecht Dürer (1471-1528) was painting round about the 1490s.

More than a hundred years after Dürer, Sir Anthony Van Dyke (1599-1641) also produced a series of water-colour landscapes, but the true line of descent for the English water-colourists is traceable more directly back to the monochrome bistre or sepia washes that such continental masters as Claude (1600-82) and Rembrandt (1606-69) used to such effect to tint many of their pen drawings. (As a matter of interest, bistre was a brown wash prepared from boiling chimney soot; sepia was derived from the ink of cuttle-fish.) Over the course of the next century or so, the monochrome wash became a generally used and successful technique in Dutch art, and it was then taken up by topographical painters in England, who found it a useful medium for dealing with qualities of atmosphere, weather and light in their pictures.

The English school of water-colourists thereafter evolved slowly as a steadily widening range of colours was introduced and as artists began to draw with their colours, as distinct from using the colours as washes or tintings on drawings already made. It may seem reasonable to speculate

Madonna and Child by Giovanni Battista Tiepolo (1696-1770). An example of pen and wash.

that the British landscape, with its great varieties of regional character and its dramatic and ever-changing contrasts in elemental conditions, fostered the growth of water-colour, which turned out to have such possibilities for capturing on paper storm and sunburst, dappled light and shade, rain on distant hills, light gleaming through mists and other features of the scenery.

According to a number of authorities, the 'father of the water-colour' was the English topographical artist Paul Sandby (1725-1809), who was employed as a draughtsman on the ordnance survey of the Scottish Highlands undertaken after the 1745 rebellion. Sandby certainly produced examples of landscape painting that were truthful and sensitive and free from picturesque exaggeration. The true revolution, however, seems to have been brought about by Thomas Girtin

(1755-1802), whose most radical innovation, say Peter and Linda Murray in their *A Dictionary of Art and Artists*, 'was the abandonment of the older monochrome underpainting in favour of a richer handling, with broad washes of strong colour often offset by dark blobs'.

Girtin's work formed the basis for the way water-colour developed during the nineteenth century, and the death of this genius at the early age of twenty-seven is still a matter for posterity to lament. He did, however, have a profound and lasting influence over his friend, J.M.W. Turner (1775-1851), who went on to extend the possibilities of water-colour until, at last, it seemed as if no effect in depicting the elements lay beyond the reach of his genius. That other major artist of the same period, John Constable (1776-1837), made a famous reference to Turner's 'airy visions, painted with tinted steam'.

Among other nineteenth-century water-colourists whose contributions might be mentioned are the founding members of the 'Norwich school', John Crome (1768-1821) and John Sell Cotman (1782-1842), together with their families and followers. Again, it was the scenery that gave them their main inspiration, even as it has, in different ways, inspired such subtle and innovative British water-colourists of the twentieth century as the brothers Paul Nash (1889-1946) and John Nash (1893-1977) as well as their contemporary John Piper (b. 1903). To bring in a contrasting figure, Edward Burra (1905-76) is an example of an English artist who used water-colour in an entirely different sort of way, to paint on a large scale and to create images that often transformed both objects and people into manifestations of the sinister and threatening.

Water-colour has never been so widely used among continental artists, but Paul Cézanne (1839-1906) turned to water-colour to carry out the late landscapes in which he moved towards his most extreme visions of abstractionism. The German Expressionist, Emil Nolde (1867-1956), also used water-colour in a startling, idiosyncratic and vital way; and the Swiss artist, Paul Klee (1879-1940), used its luminosity to convey the magical aspects of creation as he saw them in his series of imaginary landscapes and gardens.

The versatility and adaptability of water-colour are thus well accredited, and it should by now have become clear that the myth of its being a somewhat genteel or timid medium, suitable for amateurs and beginners, has no basis in either reality or common-sense. Extreme delicacy and a gem-like subtlety can, it is true, be among its attributes, but it is also

Durham Cathedral by John Sell Cotman (1782-1842). Water-colour over pencil.

fully capable of being harnessed to visions of vibrancy, even of violence. It is certainly among the most challenging and difficult of all the artistic media to master. It dries quickly, and demands nerve and spontaneity in association with a quickness of hand and eye. The speed with which water-colours dry was, in fact, among their main advantages in the first place. It meant that the artist could not only work with them in the open air, but could also pack his work away quickly in the event of a sudden shower and transport it and his equipment with ease.

Paper is a subject on its own where the background will repay some reading up, since you should become as

73

Richmond Hill and Bridge, c.1831, by J.M.W. Turner (1775-1851). Water-colour with some body colour.

familiar as possible with the papers that have been used for water-colour supports over the past two hundred years or so. The makers' watermarks not only show the correct side on which the paint should be applied (the correct side will have been treated with size to prevent it from being too readily absorbent), but can also be helpful in establishing or confirming correct dates for individual pictures.

A wide range of types and grades of paper is used for water-colour, and a water-colourist may dampen the paper before starting work on it. Paper referred to as 'cold-pressed paper' is preferred, since this is produced with a rough texture that catches the wash. The best and most highly favoured papers are the rough ones, and especially, as we have said, the handmade papers manufactured from linen rag. These represent the heavier grades, and they can be painted on to directly, whereas the lighter papers need to be dampened, stretched and then taped down on a board before they can be used. If this precaution is not taken with them, the paper will cockle as it dries.

Traditionally, papers are graded according to their weight — that is to say, to the weight that one ream (480 sheets) of the paper in question would weigh, though modern metric calculations are based on the weight of a square metre. Thus a 140-pound (300 gsm) paper is the lightest weight of paper an artist can use for water-colour without needing to dampen or stretch it; and if he wished to work on wet paper, then 240 pounds (500 gsm) would be the minimum grade he could use without stretching.

There is these days, however, one way of getting round the problem of needing to stretch lighter papers, and that is to buy them ready mounted on prepared boards; but this is a relatively recent innovation.

As we have said, pure water-colour and gouache may, as media, be mixed in a picture, but the essential distinction between the two is that gouache is opaque, not transparent. Gouache therefore has, by definition, to include a white in its palette. Its degree of opacity depends on the amount of white that is mixed in with the pigment. Gouache is also the opposite of water-colour in that an artist can work up the light on a dark background whereas water-colour on the whole involves a reverse technique.

GOUACHE

An alternative term for gouache is 'body colour', signifying that it reflects its light and does not depend on the light showing through the paint from the paper underneath. An artist can overpaint with gouache to correct errors in a way that is not possible with water-colour — a factor which has led quite unjustly to it sometimes being referred to as 'poor man's oils'.

Gouache is nothing new in art. In fact its history goes far back into antiquity, and forms of gouache technique were used by the painters of Ancient Egypt and the decorators of medieval manuscripts. The early miniaturists also used gouache, as often as not in association with pure water-colour. Gouache has also formed the backbone of the main continental water-colour tradition down to the present day, especially among Italian, Swiss and French artists of the eighteenth century, François Boucher (1703-70) being among the foremost masters of the medium. Among modern artists, Pablo Picasso (1881-1973) may be singled out as one who used gouache to great effect; and, in England, Graham Sutherland (1903-80) was an outstanding exponent.

Today we find gouache being extensively used for design and illustration work, on book jackets, record sleeves, illustrated packaging and other aspects of commercial art. This is because of the smoothness of its surfaces, which makes it especially well suited to reproduction by the standard processes of printing technology. Poster colours are often cited as a form of gouache, but these paints are far more often used in schools than they are by professional artists.

They are not really suitable for work that is intended to last over any length of time, and the quality of poster colour falls somewhat short of the dependability of gouache proper.

Painting with gouache is carried out with a similar range of brushes to those used for water-colour. The range of suitable papers that may be used, however, is a good deal more extensive, for while all the papers recommended for pure water-colour may also be used for gouache, a wider choice of options exists in that dark-toned papers can also be used. Coloured poster papers, good-quality wrapping paper, and even cardboard may similarly be utilized, so long as these have first been lightly sized with a gum solution.

TEMPERA

What are we therefore to understand by 'tempera' in the context, not of classical or antique painting, but of recent and present-day art? In its most specific sense, the term still means the egg tempera technique, where pigment is mixed with egg-yolk thinned with water to make an emulsion.

It is possible, these days, to buy tempera paints ready mixed, but the best results are still those obtained by artists who are prepared to go through the relatively troublesome process of mixing their own. In fact, although tempera was replaced in about the fifteenth century by the ascendancy of oil-painting, for a long time artists continued to use it as an alternative medium, or as a mixed medium with oils. There were a number of sporadic attempts to revive it during the nineteenth century, and William Blake (1757-1827) experimented in some of his paintings with an eccentric mix of tempera materials that turned out to be disastrously unstable. Samuel Palmer (1805-81) had better fortune, and some of his finest paintings were done in tempera and oil. On the continent, the Swiss painter Arnold Böcklin (1827-1901) and the Symbolists, Gustave Moreau (1827-98) and Gustav Klimt (1862-1918), produced important work in tempera. The more recent revival in the twentieth century is perhaps one of relatively specialist interest, but, even so, it features artists as important as Ben Shahn (1898-1969) in the United States and Edward Wadsworth (1899-1949) in Britain.

It could be that more artists would turn to tempera today if it was not for the fact of the invention of the far more convenient to use acrylics (described below). Preparing to paint in tempera is still something of an arduous procedure. Supports can consist of hardboard or chipboard, or be made of fine canvas glued on to board. Before any work at all can begin, these must first be treated front and back with artist's size. The side that is to be painted on then has to be made ready with a ground of gesso (made out of whiting, size and a small quantity of zinc white), between four and six coatings of this being the minimum required. Once the ground has dried — and it takes several days for it to do so — the surface needs sanding and finally polishing with a damp cotton cloth.

In the making of the paints themselves, a paste of pigment and distilled water is kept ready while the yolk of an egg is carefully extracted from its sac and mixed with distilled water to make the egg temper or binder. The two mixtures are finally combined in equal quantities, then tested on glass to make sure that the paint forms a skin as it dries. After this, the artist must work with speed since the tempera emulsion dries within seconds of being put on to its surface. It is also, at this stage, highly vulnerable to accidental scratching. Indeed, a tempera painting remains fragile for several months after it has been finished, and special precautions need to be taken to protect it. Although it is true that the colour values of tempera change to some extent during the process of drying, once the paint has set it will stay constant over time and not be subject to the slow darkening that inevitably comes to pass with oil-paints.

The term 'tempera' may, in practice, be extended to include egg and oil or other emulsions, the formulas for these including various oils and varnishes. Their qualities vary to some extent from pure tempera. While it is true that they do not dry so speedily, and become harder once they are dry, they remain, by comparison, rather disappointing in that they lack the best aspects of the quality of silky luminosity so prized in a true tempera finish.

MINIATURE

Within the main art media, miniature is usually given its own heading since it represents a quite distinct way of painting. Anyone who has an interest in miniatures from whatever period (they flourished from the sixteenth century through to the middle of the nineteenth century), or who is considering collecting them, will naturally be well advised to read the specialist literature on their long history.

The art of painting miniature portraits, which descends directly from the work of the illuminators of medieval manuscripts, had its first and finest flowering during the Elizabethan period in England, when its greatest master was Nicholas Hilliard (c. 1547-1619). Thereafter the demand for portable, personal and romantic likenesses continued through a variable tradition. Initially, the minia-

Portrait of An Unknown Lady. Miniature by Nicholas Hilliard (1547-1619).

turist painted mainly in a form of gouache on vellum, although, at a later period, oil on metal was adopted as an alternative method.

From about the 1700s, miniatures took on a bright new look as it became usual to paint with water-colour on a support of ivory. In parallel with this, there was also the tradition of the *enamel miniature*, strong on the continent during the seventeenth century and subsequently introduced into England. This was not, it should be noted, a true enamelling technique, but a method whereby metallic paints were lightly fused on to white enamel supports, then given an enamel glaze.

The eventual demise of the miniature finally came about in the 1850s, by which time it was already well on in its decline. The invention of photography, together with its ability to produce personal, portable, sentimentally acceptable portraits, made the miniature a superfluous art that was soon abandoned.

ACRYLIC

It is most unlikely that you will come across any examples of acrylic painting in the sale-rooms going back to an earlier date than the 1960s. Acrylic is a modern medium, mainly developed by and for artists as a side-product of the developments that have come about in modern plastics technology following the search for new industrial paints and surface finishes.

The original experiments using industrial synthetic resins to paint pictures can in fact be traced back to the 1920s and 1930s in Mexico and the United States. They were, at that stage, mainly connected with painting murals for public and commercial buildings, where the large areas of paint demanded a weather-resistant durability on a scale not hitherto dreamed of. It was only during the 1950s, though, that acrylic resins became available on a commercial scale in the United States, and had an immediate influence on a whole generation of American artists among whose leaders were Jackson Pollock (1912-56) and Mark Rothko (1903-70). By the following decade of the 1960s, acrylics were being taken up by British painters, Bridget Riley (b. 1931) and David Hockney (b. 1937) being only two examples of artists who have subsequently produced distinguished work in the new medium.

It may not be possible, with acrylic, to approach the depth and richness of surface textures that are possible with oil-paints, but the advantages possessed by these synthetic pigments are nevertheless considerable and wide-ranging. The quality of the colours in which they are manufactured has, in the general course of events, kept on steadily improving with time. They are adaptable to almost any form of support, from canvas to card and from zinc to copper. It needs only one application of a special acrylic primer to make the surface ready to take the paint, although, in the case of metal surfaces, these also need to be roughened with a fine emery paper.

The paints themselves have an elasticity that allows a painting to 'breathe'. They are considerably tougher and far less susceptible to damage or deterioration than any other sort of paint. Although it is true that they do dry very fast, overpainting presents no problems whatever. With acrylic, there are no limits to the layers of paint that the artist can place one on top of the other.

Acrylics may be thinned with water, so making possible an effect of subtleties of gradation that are not dissimilar to water-colour; or they can be used for subjects that require a strong, hard-edged finish in primary tones. It seems likely that acrylic is destined to occupy, in the years ahead, as firmly established a position in the painter's repertoire of techniques as any of the more traditional and time-tested media. It therefore follows that, in sales of more recent work, acrylics may be expected to turn up with increasing frequency as we move towards the close of the present century.

A Bigger Splash by David Hockney (b. 1937). Acrylic. 1967.

Is using an airbrush to be regarded as painting, or is it to be defined as drawing? The answer seems to be that an airbrush does both, and hence that the implement may be looked on as a sort of versatile hybrid. (Yet, having made that statement, we also need to mention that there is a specific technique known as brush drawing [see page 88 below], and this falls under the heading of drawing rather than of painting.)

An airbrush is, in fact, a fairly expensive and relatively sophisticated piece of equipment. Attached to a cylinder of compressed air, it enables an artist or designer to spray the pigments directly on to a support. Techniques exist for using, in airbrushes, all the main painting media — oil-paints, water-colours, gouache or acrylics, as well as inks and photographic dyes. One's immediate thought in the face of all this might be that nothing could sound more modern. However, evidence exists which indicates that the cave painters of prehistory had methods for spraying paint by blowing through the hollow centre of a deer's leg bone. The first patent for a modern airbrush actually dates as far back as 1893.

By the deployment of masking tape or masking fluid, it is possible to work with an airbrush to the utmost precision with regard to lines, areas of paint and gradations of colour and shading. This has tended to mean that the airbrush has been primarily an instrument for commercial artists and specialists in technical graphics. Nevertheless, the airbrush has been used by artists to paint portraits and landscapes, and if you have an interest in the art of the present day, you will soon find you can learn to recognize an airbrush technique. Its gradual blendings of tones and colours are quite distinct from the effects to be achieved by any other manner of painting.

6
DRAWINGS

PASTEL
AND
CRAYONS

We do, in fact, talk about 'painting with pastel', and pastels may simply be described as a sophisticated development of the chalks and crayons that had been in existence for centuries beforehand. The distinction possessed by pastels is that they are available in a wide range of pigments, these corresponding to the gradations of colour possible in a painter's palette. Thus an artist can, in effect, choose whether to paint or to draw with them, as he so wishes. If a linear approach to the subject is taken, then the picture is said to be drawn; but if the pastel is constructed more in terms of areas of tone and colour, then it is said to have been painted.

The invention of pastels is dated to round about the early eighteenth century, and their possibilities were seized on by the leading French artists of the day — figures such as Maurice Latour (1704-88) and Jean-Baptiste Perronneau (1715?-83), who produced work, especially portraits, of much charm and delicacy. A century later, pastels were enthusiastically taken to by a number of the French Impressionists, most notably Edgar Degas (1834-1917); and in Britain by the American-born J.A.M. Whistler (1834-1903).

The principle behind the manufacture of pastels is that powdered pigments are bound with gum or resin to hold them together in a stick, the result having a degree of friability. In this way, the artist is working with colour directly on to paper. Pastellists have a wide selection of papers available to them, graded from the moderately to the heavily grained. Clearly, the more heavily grained a paper happens to be, the more strongly it will take the pastel. Papers also come in a variety of tints, ranging from light to dark, and in various colours.

Once a pastel drawing has been finished, it remains, it needs to be emphasized, a most fragile product. The pigments can easily be damaged, like the pigments on a butterfly's wing, and a moment's rough handling may precipitate disaster. It is possible to persuade the pigments to adhere more firmly to the paper by laying a sheet of brown paper over the design and gently and firmly applying an even weight. The pigments can also be fixed with a fixative spray.

Even today, however, with the modern improved products that are available, pastellists continue to argue about the desirability of the precaution of using any sort of fixative. Some of them feel that even the best quality fixatives have, at least to some extent, a deadening effect on the life and brilliance of the colours. Because of their extreme delicacy, pastels should, when framed, always be set in a mount that will hold the glass a good quarter of an inch clear away from the surface.

Chalks, as the remote ancestors of pastels, go back into the prehistory of art, having been used by the artists of the Stone Age. They consist of soft stones or earths that are capable of giving lines or shadings of natural whites, blacks or reds. Drawing with chalks became especially popular during the Renaissance period, and they have continued to be important as a drawing medium down to the present time.

Crayons are chalk colours fixed into a stick with oil or wax binders, and wax crayons are, of course, available in a full range of colours. Unlike fragile pastels, they are robust to use, and so come into their own for teaching young children to draw. *Conté crayons*, made in the first place by the French inventor who came to be known as the 'father of the modern pencil' (see below), were originally available only in black,

Study of a Cat by F. Ernest Jackson, ARA (1873-1945). Pencil, conté and Indian ink on paper.

83

red or sepia, though today they can be obtained in every possible colour. They are sometimes used as substitutes for charcoal, but although they take well on paper, they do not have charcoal's crispness and clarity.

FROM
METAL
POINT TO
PENCIL

The *metal point* was the direct ancestor of the pencil, and metal rods or styluses, of copper or gold but most commonly of lead, were in use as drawing implements from the Middle Ages onward. To begin with, they were mainly used for preliminary sketching, for drawing in perspective lines or for architectural plans and projects. Since the impression they made was faint, they needed a prepared and slightly abrasive surface on which to make their mark effective.

Silverpoint was a development that came into especial favour for carrying out fine drawing during the fifteenth and sixteenth centuries. Since, however, it left no room whatever for error, it represented a demanding technique that was strictly for the virtuoso. For one thing, once a line had been drawn it was inerasable. For another, whatever the artist had drawn did not emerge at all clearly until the drawing had been left exposed on one side for a while, to give the traces of silver from the stylus point a chance to tarnish. The finished effect, in the hands of a master, could be one of great beauty. Some of Dürer's finest drawings, for example, were executed in silverpoint.

Graphite (otherwise known as plumbago or black-lead; hence the survival of the word 'lead' in connection with pencils, even though no true lead is used in their manufacture) had begun to be used for drawing by the close of the sixteenth century. The finest deposits of graphite in Europe were to be found in Cumberland, England, and so it came about that England emerged as the main supplier of graphite for the European artistic community. In 1693, a Deputy Governor of the Royal Mines wrote that, 'Black Lead . . . of late . . . is curiously formed into cases of Deal or Cedar, and so sold in Cases as dry Pencils.'

One of the effects of the outbreak of the French Revolution in 1789 was to cut off French artists from their leading supply of graphite, and this, in turn, prompted Nicolas-Jacques Conté (1755-1805), who was both a chemist and an artist, to experiment with mixing graphite with other materials to eke out what had come to be a scarce resource. By 1795, he had hit on a method of making mixtures of clay and graphite and firing these in a kiln. In addition, he had discovered that proportions of graphite to clay in a mixture governed the relative hardness or softness of the finished pencil. It is therefore

Bust of a warrior in profile by Leonardo da Vinci (1452-1519). Metal-point on cream-coloured, prepared surface. Italian school.

possible to relate the present-day system of grading artists' and draughtsmen's pencils from very hard (10H) to extremely soft (8B) directly back to this discovery.

Over the intervening two centuries since Conté made his innovations, pencil has become a universal medium for artists of all kinds and styles of work. It has been used in an infinite number of ways, from preliminary sketching to drawings that are highly finished, on many types of paper, card or board. It has also been used as a calculated ingredient of a picture, in association with other media, such as water-colour wash. *Coloured pencils* or *crayons*, dating from the end of the nineteenth century, are a later development of pencil work and have been widely exploited by artists in recent times. (In this context, the terms chalks and crayons, crayons and pencils, tend in general usage to become interchangeable.)

CHARCOAL

Any consideration of *charcoal* as an artistic medium takes us promptly back again to the Stone Age. The walls of the caves at Lascaux feature a number of dextrous drawings achieved with what may be assumed to have been the ends of burnt sticks. In Western art, charcoal has at times been extensively used for preliminary sketches and studies. The fresco painters of the Renaissance, for example, used charcoal to map out their designs on the walls they were about to paint, and, in a similar way, many oil-painters have used it to sketch or block in the structures of their designs on their canvases. It has also been used as a foundation for water-colour washes. The occasions on which it has been used to produce finished works of art are, however, relatively rare, despite the fact that charcoal was, for many years, turned to by teachers in art schools and colleges to instruct students in the academic practice and principles of drawing.

The heyday for charcoal as a medium in its own right probably came about during the sixteenth and seventeenth centuries, though the Impressionists of the late nineteenth century also came out with an impressive quota of work in the medium, and Vincent van Gogh used it in a notably expressive manner. In fact, charcoal holds out many possibilities for subtleties and shading of tone, and while it can be easily smudged by an accidental movement or careless handling, it can equally easily be corrected. A strongly grained paper naturally brings out its best qualities, and highlights can be produced by rubbing out with an improvised rubber of bread or putty. Where the intention is to preserve a charcoal drawing for posterity, however, it is essential for it to be fixed with a shellac or similar type of spray. Unless this precaution is taken, its life is likely to be a short one.

The traditional method for manufacturing charcoal was to burn wood in a stacked heap covered with a layer of dampened turfs to exclude the air and so ensure that the wood burned as slowly as possible. Charcoal made in this way was in demand for many uses in industry, quite apart from the artistic purposes it could be put to, and the picturesque encampments of the charcoal-burners were for centuries a feature of our woodlands — and, indeed, from time to time offered artists subjects for their paintings and drawings.

Today, industrial methods have replaced the time-honoured craft, but this has also made it possible for artists to buy processed sticks of compressed charcoal and charcoal pencils in a specified range of hardnesses. It was always recognized that different woods had different qualities once they were carbonized. Willow carbon has been the sort most usually produced, but vine carbon has been especially prized for the rich, velvety finish it is capable of producing.

The main use to which artists put charcoal nowadays is probably for drawing preliminary studies for works that they plan to carry out eventually in the medium of oil or acrylic.

PEN AND INK

The action of drawing on papyrus, parchment or paper with pointed implements designed to hold a small reservoir of ink (cut reeds or quills or, later, metal nibs), also goes far back into antiquity — at least to Ancient Egypt and China, while it was certainly also known in Classical Greece and Rome. In ancient and modern times, the base for a black ink has been the same: lamp or carbon black, although brown and sienna earths have also been used by way of common variation. Permanent black inks came to be known generally as 'India' or 'China ink' because those were the countries where the finest blacks originated.

From Leonardo in his notebooks to Rembrandt in his sketches of warm sepia and then on to Matisse and Picasso with their clear, plain lines of deceptive simplicity, pen and ink has been deployed by all the great draughtsmen as well as by innumerable lesser mortals. Nevertheless, it was most probably not until late in the nineteenth century that drawing in pen and ink was finally recognized as offering the most direct expression possible between an artist's vision and the way he directs his art. The best results have usually come into being where an artist has taken the plunge and drawn directly on to paper without relying on the presence of any underlying pencil marks. There are, incidentally, many unexpected pleasures to be gained from keeping an eye open for good examples of pen-and-ink work in the sale-rooms.

In the nature of things, except for examples from the modern schools, pen drawings will have been done with traditional nibs, using a dip technique. Artists, cartographers and draughtsmen today have a great range of reservoir pens, nibs and stylo tips at their disposal, but it is still recommended to beginners that they should practise with the traditional dip pens and nibs. A moderately heavy cartridge paper (about 60 pounds) is usually recommended for drawings in pen and ink or pen and wash, since some of the lighter papers are not so thoroughly sized and are therefore over-absorbent for this particular purpose.

BRUSH
DRAWING

Where an artist uses a brush and ink or brush and paint in an entirely linear manner, then the result is said to be a brush drawing. The earliest masters of this economical technique were the Chinese, who made no firm distinction between drawing and calligraphy, the aesthetic qualities of both being equally admired. Brush drawing, however, also came to occupy an honourable place in Western art, having evolved, during the sixteenth and seventeenth centuries, into a sophisticated and highly developed technique. During the past hundred years, recent masters, from Daumier and Degas to Matisse and Picasso, have ensured that it has kept its place in the repertoire. It should go without saying that it demands a combination of discipline with a quick dexterity as well as the ability to leave out all inessentials and state an image as its very essence.

The archetypal printmaker must be the Stone Age artist who coated the palm of his hand with pigment and then impressed it on the wall of his cave. One way and another, most printmaking methods derive from the same principle: creating an image on a surface by pressing against it a textured or incised object or material that has been primed with colour.

7
PRINTS

Most people's introduction to the concept of printmaking probably comes with the humble potato cut, beloved of playgroup supervisers and kindergarten teachers. You cut a potato in half, score a bold pattern on the flat part, dip it in wet poster paint and then print the pattern off on a sheet of paper. It is interesting and pleasing to do, but ultimately strictly limited in what may be achieved, and naturally enough, you soon grow out of it. It does, however, stand at the very foot of a ladder whose rungs are made up of increasingly complex and sophisticated methods, each one of which dramatically extends the possibilities for artistic expression.

There is another very simple method of making a repeatable image, and that is to use a stencil, enabling you to draw or paint through already cut-out shapes. The main limitation with this system is that, if you have to cut all the way round a shape, you automatically lose the middle section. Nevertheless, there are artists who have achieved some notable designs by using ingenious sequences of stencils. It is a principle, too, that has in recent years been expanded into the techniques of screen printing (see page 100 below) and thus transformed in the process.

Printmaking today falls under four main headings: the relief methods, the intaglio methods, the surface methods and the stencil methods. This is therefore the order in which we will consider them in the following pages, but before we do so there are certain points that need to be re-emphasized.

Collecting and trading in antique or period prints of all kinds is a hazardous field and itself a specialist area in the art market. The beginner must therefore feel his or her way most carefully and combine much background reading with direct observation, slowly getting to know which are the true rarities and the items of genuine interest, and distinguishing these from examples whose values are mainly one of curiosity or that are too common to stand a significant profit mark-up on resale.

The usual run of topographical prints, for example, are likely to have a slightly higher value when sold in the areas they depict. Therefore, if you bought prints of Dorset in Lincolnshire, say, you might be able to show a profit if you then took them to Dorset to dispose of them. But unless you already have a known outlet for such material in Dorset, it seems doubtful whether it will pay you to go to all the trouble. The gist of what we are saying here is really that there are no flukes of fortune involved in the matter of prints. It takes a practised eye to pick out and identify the items of merit.

So far as the collector is concerned, the modern print seems to represent a safer ground since the standardization of editions and the conventions involved leave far less room for ambiguities. The number of copies in an edition, the number in the sequence that this print represents, the artist's signature are all guarantees for the collector that the level of their availability is under control. If collecting is your game, then the modern print holds out many fascinating prospects, and you can expect your collection to mature in value over time, especially if you are shrewd in the work you go for. It is not, however, an area that is likely to produce instant profits.

When you are looking at exhibitions of prints, you may notice that some, instead of being numbered, are called 'Artist's proofs'. All that this means is that each is one of the few copies that the artist pulled for his own reference or use over and above the numbers printed for the edition. There are also prints that are specified as 'Signed on the plate', which simply means that the artist's signature or initials have been incorporated within the design. Where this has been done, it usually means that, for some reason or other, it was decided to produce the print in a general rather than a limited edition.

Relief Methods

WOODCUTS AND LINOCUTS

The relief methods for the making of prints may be said to belong to the most straightforward group, including, as they do, the *woodcut* and the *linocut* as main examples. When an artist makes a woodcut or a linocut, he is naturally working with a reverse image of how the picture or impression will eventually appear. He is also, in effect, creating a printing block by cutting away the parts that he does not need to have showing in the finished image or design. The areas or lines that go to make the impression are thus left outstanding on the block, and it is these that take the printing ink (applied by roller or pad). Printing the image on to paper (which should be unsized and therefore absorbent) is then achieved under light pressure in a press. By making sure that the register of the blocks is precise, it is possible to build up designs of more than one colour, and the results can in fact become quite sophisticated in the hands of a skilled craftsman. The inks used are usually oil-based, although the Japanese tradition of woodblock printing was founded on water-colour.

In the present day, there are other relief methods which have come into vogue, such as utilizing cardboard or sheets of plastic or metal. Even attaching leaves or textured materials and other *objets trouvés*, such as buttons or coins, to a flat surface has been adopted as a way of creating a block from which a print can be made.

WOOD-ENGRAVING

Linocuts, woodcuts and their close relations have, on the whole, lent themselves to broad, boldly based designs, since any fine lines are likely to be broken, compressed or otherwise distorted as soon as only a few copies have been printed off. A great advance in subtlety became possible with developments in *wood-engraving*, a technique that exploits the enormous gain in strength which is to be obtained by working on hardwood blocks at right angles to the grain. The wood is here cut away with a burin (the main tool used by engravers), and the fineness of line and the details of light or shade are fully capable of rivalling those in any other form of engraving. Examples of the medium tend to be small, even miniaturist in scale, this reflecting the fact that boxwood is regarded as the best material for the purpose.

Wood-engraving of a grey-lag goose by Thomas Bewick (1753-1828)

Some of the most famous and familiar wood-engravings are those of Thomas Bewick (1753-1828), who produced them as illustrations and vignettes to illustrate his own books on natural history — now, of course, highly sought after in the antiquarian book trade. The durability of these engraved blocks when used for printing purposes was quite phenomenal. Bewick's books went through many editions, and he was once able to calculate that a delicate view of Newcastle-upon-Tyne, cut at the request of a newspaper proprietor some years before, had been used to print off more than 9 million individual impressions in the newspaper concerned without having registered any obvious signs of wear and tear.

RELIEF
ETCHING

We deal with etching below, under 'Intaglio Methods', but *relief etching* is a kind of reverse etching method that exploits a relief technique. It has been used mainly since the eighteenth century, the design being drawn on to a copper or zinc plate with an acid-resistant varnish. When this plate is then immersed in an acid bath, the design will be left standing in relief where the varnish has protected it. The main snag of relief etching is that there are limitations to the number of copies obtainable before the relief begins to betray signs of wearing down.

Intaglio Methods

In the parlance of the art world, 'intaglio' simply means the opposite of 'cameo'. Where, with cameo, the image is raised, it is recessed with intaglio. This conveys the principle of intaglio: the image is printed, not from what stands out on the plate, but from what is actually recessed within it.

The most usual forms of prints produced in this way are the line engraving, the drypoint and the etching. In all of these, the principle applied is the same: the plate is first inked, then wiped clean, so that only the incisions or scorings are left holding any ink. Damp paper laid on the plate then takes up the image under heavy pressure applied in a copperplate press.

The metals used to make intaglio plates have usually been copper or zinc, although, more recently, mild steel or aluminium have replaced them to some extent, copper being an expensive commodity nowadays. Whatever the metal used happens to be, however, it will express its own characteristics in the finished print, and these are details that the expert eye will come to recognize and distinguish, given some time and practice.

With *line engraving*, the design is cut directly into the surface of the plate — in other words, is engraved — with a sharp burin or graver. Copper is still the most recommended metal for this kind of direct engraving, but the technique is a highly demanding one in the skills of control and the prior experience and knowledge of its possibilities that it requires. A largely commercial development of this method was *steel engraving*, which remained in use throughout the first half of the nineteenth century for making editions of prints on a large and popular scale. The main characteristic of a steel engraving is that it has a very hard-edged and precise image.

LINE
ENGRAVING

Eighteenth-century engraving of George III.

DRYPOINT

Drypoint is a variant intaglio method where the design is scratched on to the plate with a needle that has a hardened or diamond point. The scratch marks produce a burr that stands up slightly above the surface of the metal, and this has the effect of making the lines slightly fuzzed and hence softer and subtler than those to be observed in line engraving. Unfortunately, the burr soon begins to flatten out as soon as copies are printed off, and therefore strict limits apply to the number of good copies of a drypoint print that are obtainable. Giving the plate a steel coating by electrolysis can lengthen its life quite considerably, but drypoint has most often been used in combination with other techniques.

ETCHING

In *etching* itself, the surface of the metal plate is initially covered with a thin layer of wax. The design is then drawn on the wax with a sharp point that exposes the metal underneath, and the plate is placed in an acid bath. The longer the plate is left in the bath, the deeper will the acid bite, and hence the timing of the process is an important element in the final effect being aimed for. Where only light impressions are needed, the plate will be removed from the bath to have these areas varnished over before being reimmersed to bring up the stronger, darker areas (a tactic known as 'stopping out').

So far as is known, the technique of etching began some time in the early sixteenth century. It probably reached its most illustrious peak as an artistic medium with the series of etchings produced by Rembrandt, who also, incidentally, tended to work on his etched plates in drypoint. Throughout the following three hundred years, etching has maintained its popularity among the other methods of printmaking.

A word needs to be said here about what is meant by 'state' in connection with etchings. To put it at its simplest, the first state is that where the etcher pulls his first proofs and checks them for any changes he may wish to make. If he should institute a change, then the next printed result will be the 'second state'; and so on, according to however many changes are made before the artist is satisfied.

SOFT-GROUND ETCHING

An interesting variant on etching technique is provided by *soft-ground etching*, where the plate is initially covered with a layer of soft, usually black wax. A sheet of thin paper is then laid over the top, and on to this the artist draws the design. When the paper is lifted off the wax, it brings with it the wax where the drawing has been impressed into the surface. The plate is then etched in an acid bath in the usual

Fishing Fleet by William Lionel Wyllie (1851-1931). Signature in pencil lower left margin. Etching.

way. A finished soft-ground print, with its soft texture, has a look that seems closer in appearance to a pencil or chalk drawing than to a normal etching.

AQUATINT

Aquatint is a process, formerly quite popular, that has been through something of a revival in recent years. It is called aquatint, not because water is used in the process of making it, but because the finished print bears a resemblance to a water-colour drawing. The aquatint image is built out of tones rather than lines, this being achieved by initially dusting a powdered resin on to the surface of the plate. When the plate is heated, the drops of resin then fuse to the metal and the design can be worked on to the plate with stop-out varnish. The final image is brought about in stages by a sequence of immersions in an acid bath.

The artist who, above all others, stretched the expressive and creative possibilities of aquatinting to their limits was Francisco Goya (1746-1828), who used it both in a pure form and as a mixed media with etching, seemingly finding that it was capable of conveying some of the remarkable qualities of his own imagination.

SUGAR-LIFT
AQUATINT

A more recent development of aquatinting is the *sugar-lift aquatint*, which, it so happens, does use water at one stage of its process. In this method, the design is drawn boldly and directly on to the plate with a solution of sugar and Indian ink. The surface is then varnished. Simply soaking the plate in water will then lift off the sugar mixture and leave exposed those areas that are to be aquatinted in an acid bath.

MEZZOTINT

While *mezzotints* are usually thought of as belonging to the seventeenth to the nineteenth centuries, working in this medium never became entirely defunct and some printmakers have turned to it again in recent times. The tech-

Portrait of Mrs Finlay by Henry Macbeth Raeburn (1860-1947) after Sir Henry Raeburn (1756-1823). Colour mezzotint.

nique, invented in Holland in the 1640s, evolved into a procedure where the engraver worked from dark to light, starting with a plate that had been heavily burred and pitted all over its surface by an instrument known as a 'rocker'. The design could then actually be formed by scraping away the burr and finally burnishing the metal to bring up the lights and half-lights. Wherever a special contrast of light or dark was required in a finished print, this was therefore an ideal medium, and the richness of its velvety tones came to be much admired. For several generations of art lovers, mezzotint versions in popular prints were the main access they had to famous paintings by many artists, from Reynolds to Constable.

Crayon or *pastel manner* and *stipple engraving* were two techniques that were used almost exclusively for popular reproductions, and then only during the eighteenth and nineteenth centuries. In a present-day context, they may be regarded as extinct in the platemaker's repertoire. The crayon or pastel manner called on a battery of etching needles, scrapers and burnishers to create a fair imitation of drawing in chalk or pastel. In a similar way, stipple engraving was applied by minute dots to outline the subject being reproduced, the engraver then going on to work up the tonal areas. Clearly the introduction of half-tones and other developments in illustrative printing rendered both these minor branches of craftsmanship obsolete.

CRAYON AND PASTEL MANNER/ STIPPLE ENGRAVING

Surface Methods

The surface or planographic methods of printmaking all derive from the principles exploited by *lithography*. This is a technique, adopted on a large scale in the printing industry today, that utilizes the fact that grease and water are incompatible.

LITHOGRAPHY

The inventor of the lithograph was a German playwright, Aloys Senefelder (1771-1834), who one day, purely out of convenience, happened to use a grease crayon to jot down a laundry list on a piece of stone. It at once occurred to him that, if he were to etch away the stone, the writing would be left standing up in relief and so would constitute a printing block. He was, at the time, actually looking for a cheap way of printing the texts of his plays.

A couple of years of experiment brought him to the realization that the etching part of the process was, in fact, unnecessary. You could, as he saw, print the image direct

Mr Jorrocks: 'Come hup! I say. You ugly brute!' Coloured lithograph by John Leech (1817-1864) published by Agnew, 1865. (From *Hunting Incidents of the Noble Science.*)

from the flat stone, and here was how you might do it. First you could carefully and thoroughly smooth and level off the surface of the stone block, and then draw on it your design in greasy ink or pencil. Once this greasy image had been fixed with chemicals, the stone could be rinsed off with water. Now the stone would, where it was damp, repel any printing-ink that had a grease base; but the same ink would adhere to the greasy image itself. It would then be possible to print off the image directly on to a sheet of paper in a press.

In his writings and teachings, Senefelder laid down the basis for all future developments of the method he invented. Its value was quickly recognized by leading artists, who saw in it the possibilities for a directness and spontaneity possessed by no other printmaking technique. From the aged Goya, to Daumier, Degas, Toulouse-Lautrec, Braque and Picasso, and on down to the present time, the lithograph has been taken up as a medium that allows for a particular freshness and flexibility of expression.

In the printing industry, lithography has undergone some highly sophisticated technical developments, and litho printing is now carried out on the most modern commercial presses with flexible zinc plates that can be attached to the printing rollers. For many artists, too, zinc and other metals have replaced the traditional stone blocks. There is always the danger of the stone splitting if slightly too much pressure is applied during the printing. Moreover, grinding the stone, either in preparation or for re-use, remains a laborious proceeding. Nevertheless, where the objective is to gain the subtlest possible effects, then stone is still regarded as the best material for making a lithographic plate.

Multi-coloured prints are made, as with linocuts or woodcuts, by preparing a separate block for each main colour, while bearing in mind, if necessary, the effects of overlay (for example, yellow on blue gives green). The register for each block obviously needs to be marked with great precision.

In theory, a lithographic block can go on producing impressions into infinity. In practice, a limit will usually be set to the edition, as with other prints, and the stone will then be scored through or re-ground. It can happen that you will come across an edition that is deliberately unlimited, but here the artist will have produced it for the pleasure of a wider public rather than for the collector, and it will probably also be unsigned, or signed or initialled 'on the stone'.

MONOPRINT OR MONOTYPE

A cousin of the surface method is the *monoprint* or *monotype*, which, as its name implies, will be produced in no more than a unique copy, or perhaps two copies at the very most. What, you may well ask, could prompt an artist into wishing to produce only a single copy of something that has to be printed anyway? The answer is to obtain a result that is quite unlike and distinct from a direct piece of painting. To make a monoprint, the image is painted on glass, metal or plastic, and then, while still wet, printed off on to paper in a printmaker's press.

Stencil Methods

Stencils possess, as we have said, their limitations as ways of making prints, but also their possibilities. As the *Oxford Companion to Art* concisely puts it, 'from the aesthetic point of view [the stencil's] very simplicity and sharpness of outline may become major virtues'. Stencils have also sometimes been used in combination with linocuts or woodcuts for introducing defined areas of colour; and in France there is a tradition of stencil work (*pochoir*) that developed the device for book illustration in limited or high-quality editions.

SCREEN-
PRINTING

The outstanding evolution in the stencil principle in modern times has been that of *screenprinting*, sometimes called *silk-screen printing* or *serigraphy* or even *sieve printing*, the first use for which dates from the late 1930s. Since then it has, with its variant methods and improvements, placed in the hands of artists a flexible and versatile device that is capable of making prints in a great variety of styles and sizes and that can accommodate either broad design or intricate detail with equal ease. As with lithography, there is, in theory, no limit to the numbers of any one print that may be produced, but in practice the usual restrictions of a specified edition will apply.

The screen itself is of fine natural or synthetic textile mesh, stretched to tension on a frame. Stencils may be cut from paper or sheets of plastic, or they may, more commonly, take the form of liquid fillers. Where cut stencils are concerned, these will be stuck to the underside of the screen. With fillers, on the other hand, the artist is enabled to work directly on to a screen with a solution of varnish or glue. The principle is that, wherever ink is able to penetrate the mesh, then it is possible for an image to be formed. An artist will therefore work either to a negative method (stopping out those areas where it is required that the ink should make no impression) or to a positive method (painting in lines or stippling areas, but using waxy or oily materials that can be washed out with turpentine from an overall coating of filler).

Screenprinting can be done on any paper that is suitable for reproducing the image to a satisfactory standard and is compatible with the saleable quality of the final product. For the process of printing, the screen is folded down so that it lies flat on the paper on the printing table and the ink is pressed through the mesh by drawing a rubber squeegee across the surface of the screen. The inks used may be related to water-colour, to oil or acrylic, and by using a series of stencils (a separate one for each colour) a multiplicity of colour shadings and effects can be built up. It is also possible to make photo-stencils (stencils incorporating actual photographs) by coating the mesh of the screen with a film of light-sensitive emulsion — a technique that has led to the inclusion of documentary images in some of the modern schools of printmaking, Robert Rauschenberg (b. 1925) in the United States being a notable example.

All pictures are vulnerable, and certain pictures are more so than others. The extent of their vulnerability depends, naturally enough, on the materials from which they were constructed in the first place. Works of art have many enemies, and these can range from careless handling to unsympathetic treatment or even unsuitable conditions in the environment where they happen to be kept. Even a speck of dust, wrote Helmut Ruhemann in his *magnum opus* on the principles of restoration, *The Cleaning of Pictures*, 'may become a small focus for condensation of atmospheric moisture, and certainly dampness improves the chances for a surface to hold any grime that comes its way'.

8

CARE

AND

REPAIR

Heat or light, humidity or dryness, atmospheric pollution or attacks by insects, impurities in paint or paper, technical shortcomings on the part of the original artist in the way materials were used to paint the picture, and also in mounting or framing — any one of these may number among the factors capable of undermining the integrity of a painting, drawing or print. The consequences will be obvious: its life is in danger of being shortened and its value and desirability are both placed at risk.

Nothing lasts for ever, and time itself is rarely on the side of any work of art. As George L. Stout states in a classic handbook, *The Care of Pictures* (1948):

> As soon as a picture is finished it starts to *deteriorate*. Those first few days or months are the only time in its whole history when its condition is perfect. The change in it will be produced by inevitable circumstances and by chance acting on the materials from which it is made. The rate of change will depend a good deal on the relation of the picture's surface to conditions in the air, on its ability to withstand dust, wear, injurious gases, light and dampness.

The way in which pictures are hung on the walls and presented as well as how they are stored are therefore matters of vital importance for anyone who has the responsibility of handling and caring for them. We have, for instance, in general come to take central-heating as a routine feature of home life, without ever thinking of the toll it may be taking of our art treasures unless it is properly controlled. Ruhemann records how, at an earlier stage of the history of collecting in the United States, many imported masterpieces:

> quickly began to deteriorate through the totally different climatic conditions, extremes of heat and cold and the inordinate overheating of most houses and museums. It was many years before adequate air-conditioning plants began to be installed in the museums. In the meantime the most common ailment of pictures, the flaking of the paint, became very prevalent . . .

Whether they are hung on the wall or stored, the pictures in any permanent collection should be inspected at regular intervals — at least once a year — for signs of trouble or deterioration. Many collectors of pictures keep their favourites on the walls in the same position for years on end and never give the matter an instant's consideration. It never occurs to them to think in terms of keeping a reserve of pictures in store so that their collection can be changed about from time to time. Yet it takes only a small amount of thought to show how it could be a matter of wisdom and common-sense to do so.

A delicately toned water-colour, drawing or print that has been hung in a position where it catches direct sunlight, or even where the light reaching it from outside is no more than moderately strong, may be found to have suffered, slowly and imperceptibly, an irreparable fading in its pigments over the course of the years. There are, indeed, certain museum curators who would hold that any light strong enough to view a delicate picture by is going, by definition, to be too intense for the health of the picture concerned.

The way we travel and store those pictures that we do not hang on the walls also needs some conscious thought. When carrying pictures away from an auction or transporting them for exhibition or to show to clients, then the way they are handled and loaded into any vehicle is obviously important. The boots or backs of most dealers' cars have a plentiful supply of worn-out sheets and blankets, old newspapers and straps, so that packing can be improvised and pictures cushioned and anchored to ensure that they do not slide around and buffet each other during the course of a journey. They should be laid flat on a well-protected soft base so that they cannot slide or tip if the car lurches or stops suddenly. If you have an estate type of car, it gives an obvious advantage since it is much easier to load and unload than a saloon whose boot and back seats are not really designed with the transportation of pictures in mind. It is also possible to buy special packing materials with built-in cushioning with which you can wrap each picture individually.

Unframed prints, drawings or water-colours should always be kept in portfolios, laid flat on a firm surface and with layers of (acid-free) tissue paper between each item. Framed pictures of every kind need to be stored in compartmented racks (quite simple to design and build) where they may be kept upright, but without cramming too many pictures into each compartment and so creating a build-up of weight. Where pictures do need to be leant against each other, they should be arranged so that it is the frames that take up any of the strain. With canvases, care is needed to make sure that no sharp corners are creating pressure on any part of the painting and that there is no chance of surfaces being accidentally rubbed or scraped as you lift pictures in and out. The racks should be positioned where the lighting is subdued and the atmosphere cool and well-ventilated.

On every occasion when you handle any unframed, unmounted print, drawing or painting that has been pro-duced on a paper support, then, no matter how carefully you handle it and regardless of whether you wash your hands beforehand, you are going to be causing the work a minuscule yet positive measure of harm. This is because the paper will absorb acid from the natural secretions carried by the skin of your fingers, acid being among the prime enemies of all works of art that rely on any sort of paper base. The habit observed by members of earlier schools of print connoisseurs of keeping pairs of white cotton gloves both to wear themselves and to offer guests in their libraries or collection rooms when showing off acquisitions, was certainly no precious affectation. These people were only too aware of how the effects of damage are likely to build up with repeated handling, and present-day collectors who possess portfolios of valued material would be well advised to follow their example.

It follows from these observations that care in handling and care in storing, positioning and lighting, figure promi-nently among the first principles of conservation for works of art. Nevertheless, in the midst of the best of intentions and circumstances, mishaps may still occur alongside the natural ravages of time, and this raises the question of techniques for restoration — restoration being taken to imply the reinstating of a picture to a condition that matches the artist's original intention as closely as it is possible to make it. Helmut Ruhemann, who could lay claim to being both a pioneering and, at times, a controversial figure during the many years he spent as Consultant Restorer to the National Gallery in London, arrived at five definitions for the measures involved in the principles of restoration. These were, he stated in his standard book on the subject, *The Cleaning of Paintings*:

1. Preservation of sound paintings.
2. Treatment of ailing paintings.
3. Cleaning.
4. Retouching.
5. Re-varnishing.

Moreover, he said, these objectives often appeared under two other headings: on the one hand, consolidation, by which he meant the 'technical or constructional'; and, on the other, the aesthetic or artistic. Thus we can see how restoration may at certain times be a perfectly simple, straightforward procedure, but how it may at others involve, even for the most experienced cleaner and restorer, various complex questions that come to be unavoidably caught up with a degree of informed guesswork and areas of debate, even of ethics.

The question of whether or not an amateur should ever attempt to learn and apply any of the techniques for repair or restoration is one to take us directly into a controversial area. A great majority of experts would state unhesitatingly and categorically, 'Never!' They have, we may be sure, some very good reasons for their reaction. 'Far more damage has probably been done by enthusiastic amateur cleaners than by professional restorers,' wrote Ruhemann with feeling. The problem is that there are certain unpredictable things that can happen during the course of the simplest operation that only a trained and experienced restorer will be able to recognize and deal with. The views expressed here are therefore in line with those of the experts, and our recommendation is that cleaning and restoration should, in all their aspects, be left in the hands of those who are properly trained to deal with them. The roles of dealer and restorer should invariably be kept distinct from each other.

Even the most skilled practitioner needs to bear constantly in mind how a single wrong or ill-informed move is capable of spoiling the most pleasant, harmless picture beyond redemption and leaving its owner with a tragic piece of wreckage that has arbitrarily ceased to be of any value or interest to anyone. It is perfectly true that even some of the world's great masterpieces have, in times gone by, found themselves being submitted to hair-raising hazards at the hands of well-intentioned yet ill-informed 'expert' restorers. The history of art is hardly short of horror stories and object lessons to carry the point home. In the entry for 12 November 1919 in his *Diary of an Art Dealer*, René Gimpel records a conversation he once held with a fellow dealer, Nathan Wildenstein:

> I told Wildenstein I had gone that afternoon to Mme X, who has begun cleaning one of my primitives, and I added that she's very inept. 'Why, yes,' said Wildenstein, 'it's she who cleaned Spencer's *Flora* [the painting by Rembrandt, formerly in the possession of Lord Spencer]. She made the yellow flowers on the hat disappear. The Duveens, who had given it her to devarnish, said they were fake, but it isn't so; it's that woman who made the yellow go, since yellow can't stand up to a bad cleaning. Twenty-five years ago I had a picture of fruit including a cut melon. Before my eyes a woman restorer cleaned it and the melon began to dissolve as if under someone's teeth.'

There is a dictum which holds that it is only possible to achieve restoration through destruction. Cleaning the surface of an oil-painting, removing old and darkened varnish to replace it with a fresh, clear surface is one thing. Camouflaging a mended tear in a canvas or covering up where a flake of paint has fallen away is yet another. Overpainting adds yet a further dimension and opens up fresh possibilities for the development of arguments about unscrupulous practice or overstepping the limits of whatever is felt to be acceptable. From the moment a restorer begins to overpaint any of an artist's original brush strokes, a whole fresh set of value judgements may come into play, these including fashionable and therefore anachronistic and subjective ideas about how the painting will have looked when it was new at a date which may quite possibly go back over several centuries.

The controversial aspect of these arguments therefore comes to centre on ideas about the original tonal values of antique paints and varnishes and to raise questions of whether the over-zealous cleaning, and what is seen as the 'restoration' of old masters, may not, in fact, be more appropriately described as distortions in the cause of bending their effect to match up with modern notions of what they ought to look like. While such approaches may seem to make a masterpiece more accessible, it is not irrelevant to ask whether they can only do so at what may be defined as a risky kind of cost. The arguments surrounding these questions are likely to go on being heard for many years ahead, and it is not our intention to become at all closely caught up in them. The one thing we may say with confidence is that, in cases where extreme damage has been suffered through the accidental disasters of, say, fire and flood, it seems that being able to see a restored masterpiece is better than having no masterpiece surviving in any form.

In the whole long history of painting, Leonardo da Vinci's *The Last Supper* must surely stand among the most sensational and unlikely of survivors. The subject of Christ with his disciples, seated at the last supper, had provided a major challenge to the practitioners of Christian art from its very beginning. Leonardo had spent in the region of fifteen years in his own preparations for tackling the subject and working out an original approach to the problem of how to vitalize the essentially pedestrian image of thirteen men seated together at table. The sad thing was that, when he finally came to confront the refectory wall in the Dominican monastery of Santa Maria delle Grazie in Milan, where his patron, Ludovica Sforza, decreed the enterprise should be carried out, the actual methods he used were less well tested than the artistic solutions he sought to apply.

To start with, he worked on a surface made of an experimental compound based on pitch, and then, between the years 1495 and 1498, laboured to create his masterpiece on this unsuitable ground. What was more, he tested out another speculative mixture of the paints themselves in his efforts to break free from the straitjacket of the established fresco technique of painting on to wet plaster. Nevertheless he produced what must have been an astonishing result, the refectory where the Dominican monks took their meals seeming to merge with the room in which Christ and his disciples enacted a supreme moment of destiny. Yet a further major problem existed in that the building itself was liable to suffer from flooding. Given this fact, together with the mural's unorthodox backing of pitch and mastic and its experimental paintwork, it hardly comes as a surprise to learn that it began to flake alarmingly almost immediately after it was finished. By the time Vasari paid a visit to view the painting in 1556, he could make out nothing of its images 'except a muddle of blots'.

Leonardo da Vinci's
Last Supper. (Left)
Detail of Christ's
head showing the
fragmentary nature
of the painting,
which is in the
Santa Maria delle
Grazie, Milan.

Over the succeeding centuries, the great original was patched and restored time and time again by hands of varying competence or limitation. In 1901, the Italian poet Gabriele d'Annunzio bade it a positively last farewell with his 'Ode on the Death of a Masterpiece'. Even so, many years of skilful and meticulous restoration then managed once again to salvage the wreckage of the painting, and happily it was protected by sandbags from the main blast of the Allied bombs which reduced most of the refectory building to a heap of rubble in 1943.

Immediately after the Second World War, the refectory was rebuilt and the work of restoration proceeded again; and finally, in the later 1980s, a further long-term programme was set in motion to realize an ultimate act of conservation, bringing the very latest scientific techniques to bear on distinguishing, preserving and bringing into prominence every minute scrap of paint that could possibly be identified as belonging to Leonardo's original work. The picture we know today may be a spectral ruin of what existed on the refectory wall at the start of its life, but it is still possible to glimpse and sense its power and beauty.

Another large-scale restoration project continuing during recent years has been the cleaning of Michelangelo's frescoes on the ceiling of the Sistine Chapel in the Vatican, Rome. As Sir John Pope-Hennessy said in an article in the *New York Review of Books* (8 October 1987), written as a reply to the fears of critics of the venture, 'The cleaning of the Sistine ceiling is the most important piece of fresco restoration that has ever been attempted, because the ceiling is almost certainly the greatest painting that has ever been produced.'

The dual purpose has been to make the frescoes secure for the future and to remove the blackening effects arising from the candles and oil lamps that were kept burning within the body of the chapel in former times and which have naturally created an obscuring surface layer. As the process of cleaning has reached completion over certain areas, the splendour of what it has revealed has been breathtaking.

But these ventures, like the long-term programmes of salvage, rescue and restoration that were set in motion following the disastrous floods in Florence in 1966, are in general acknowledged as necessities and models for the self-effacing and painstaking use of modern skills in the service of art. The main focuses for controversy and argument emerge whenever we come up against the less obviously essential approaches to cleaning, restoration and conservation: in other words, where the approach begins to overlap with what might be called a cosmetic view.

It could well be that, in an age where so many major museums have their own laboratory and sophisticated technological facilities, there has been what can only be described as a craze for restoration: a marked tendency towards 'overcleaning' with sometimes calamitous results. However, while it is necessary to be broadly informed on the various pros and cons of the arguments involved here, such an inquiry is not, as we say, the purpose of the present text. Our main concern, of course, needs to be with the best way of recognizing and dealing with those problems most likely to be encountered among paintings, prints and drawings in the lower and less illustrious reaches of the art market — the kind of work in the provincial sale-rooms in which we have a particular interest.

The whole practice and development of the restoration and conservation of pictures has tended to centre on oil-painting for two reasons. First, as we have seen, the oil easel-painting represented the central line of tradition and progress in Western art during all the centuries following the Renaissance. The vast majority of important works of art have therefore been carried out in this medium. Secondly, as we have also seen, the way an oil-painting is built up from the many materials used in its creation gives it a uniquely complex structure. There is, to put it another way, simply so much that is capable of going wrong. The trouble may lie with the timber of the stretcher, with the canvas backing itself, with the way the paint was applied and the actual layers of paint, or with the varnish that gives the picture its surface glaze.

The signs that point to the effects of ageing, accident or mistreatment should all in time become evident to the practised eye. To begin with the topmost layer of all — the varnish — the technique of cleaning off old, darkened and discoloured varnish and applying a fresh coat is one of the most common aspects of picture restoration. This does not, however, mean to say that an old varnish is necessarily any great disadvantage when it comes to buying a painting to dispose of, since the dealers may regard its presence as a reassuring sign that here they have a picture that has been neither on the market for several years nor previously tampered with. It will be perfectly reasonable for you to buy a painting as a 'dark-brown picture' and to sell it on as such. The responsibility for a decision on whether to provide such an oil-painting with a brand-new surface sparkle may then simply be handed on to your dealer client, who will judge

THE CARE AND PRESERVATION OF OILS

how much giving it a clean will affect the price-tag he is able to put on it when he displays it in his window.

There was, in Victorian times and earlier, a positive vogue for using certain varnishes which used bitumen to build in their antique finishes deliberately. It has to be remembered that Victorian artists had never seen a cleaned picture and so did not realize that bright colours had been used in the past. It was therefore perhaps natural for them to use a dark varnish whenever they were aspiring to an 'Old Master' effect. Helmut Ruhemann, however, is merciless in the scorn he pours on these 'golden glow' or 'gallery tone' varnishes, while severely criticizing the 'fallacy that many old masters applied or desired a "patina to improve their pictures"'.

> A great old master, after proudly putting the last touch to his work, would hardly expect Time to finish or improve it. Nor would he be likely to have said to his patron in delivering the commission: 'This is not quite right yet, but in ten or twenty or perhaps fifty years it will look much better and more as I want it.'

But Ruhemann, of course, is mainly concerned to promote his own principles of picture restoration, and, as we have said, to set out to clean and revarnish every period oil-painting in sight is not in itself an especially virtuous principle from the point of view of the dealer. There will undoubtedly be cases where leaving well alone is the best course by far to pursue. Where a painting is going to benefit from a general revarnishing, then this needs to be done out of a carefully considered policy towards that particular painting. Moreover, in the case of the Victorian artists who deliberately sought to darken their paintings with special varnishes, we should presumably restore them in line with their original intentions, however misguided we may feel these to have been.

The phenomenon of 'bloom' in varnishes was one that was encountered far more in the past than it is today, simply because the synthetic resins used to manufacture modern varnishes are not as a rule prone to its development. You may still encounter the condition, however, in older paintings that still have their original coatings of varnish made from natural resins. It is easily recognized as a patch of whitish film, usually affecting no more than a small portion of the picture, and the usual cause is thought to be moisture in the atmosphere. Routine cases, which are by far the most commonly occurring ones, may sometimes be dealt with by simply rubbing the affected area with a silk handkerchief or a swab of cotton wool slightly moistened with distilled water, though if the patches of bloom are more tenacious they may need treating with a wax varnish. There are occasions, however, when blooming indicates a more persistent and deep-seated problem that may be attributed to condensation having formed at the time when the original varnish was drying or to moisture having got in with its original ingredients. A painting which shows any sign of suffering from this sort of bloom will certainly require being treated at the hands of a professional restorer.

As we have already emphasized, readers of this book will search in vain for any recommendation to help amateurs in general feel relaxed about trying their hand at even the most basic pieces of first-aid in picture conservation. The trip-wires of inflicting irreversible damage on a painting of any value through inexperience and ignorance spread themselves in all directions, and picture restoring is one area where learning from experience can mean paying for lessons most expensively in terms of ruined works of art. From time to time one picks up pieces of folklore suggesting how, say, it is possible for amateurs to clean paintings by using sliced onions or certain proprietary brands of cleaning fluid. Be firm in resisting all such tempting and attractive notions designed to skirt the necessity of paying a restorer his fee. The odds will be that such methods can do nothing but harm, and they certainly will not have originated from a scientifically informed source.

Those who set out to master the skills of picture restoration need to prepare their ground carefully and to be practical individuals capable of maintaining a realistic assessment at every stage of how far their skills extend and what still lies beyond their abilities. They are the people to whom we may turn once we have a problem in need of a solution. First, however, you have to buy your problem, or avoid buying it as the case may be. The skills that you need to develop are therefore those of being able to recognize, as you inspect a canvas in an auction-room, where conservation or restoration is likely to be needed before the picture can be sold on to any other purchaser, and to assess the extent and nature of the work this is going to involve and hence whether it will be worth your while to take on the responsibility.

To begin with the most basic part of the structure, the *stretcher*, the most obvious indications of trouble to watch out for would be those of an infestation of woodworm. If there should be any sign of worm-holes, inspect these carefully with a magnifying-glass. A few very old ones may be nothing to worry about; they may just show that the trouble has been successfully dealt with in the past. The smallest fresh grain of powdered wood, on the other hand, will show you that the worm is active. What is more, there will be no sure way for you to judge the extent of the damage and infestation since the material of the canvas covers and conceals so much of the wood. Wherever you see fresh worm-holes you will be wise to make the assumption that the canvas needs to be remounted on to a new stretcher.

While you still have the painting turned about to examine the back, you should also see if you can manage to spot any signs of excess rust where iron tacks are beginning to rot through the canvas. If this should be starting to happen, then all the old tacks may need to be removed and the canvas restretched on to the stretcher, preferably with tacks made of copper on this occasion.

If you do find any active woodworm signs in the stretcher, then the odds are that it will also have got into the *frame*. It goes without saying that you will also need to check the frame for any signs of this sort of unwelcome intrusion, although treating a frame on its own for a mild case of woodworm may not be too drastic an operation. In any case, a serious infestation in a frame will be quite obvious to the eye, and it is unlikely that any auctioneer of repute will allow a painting into his sale-room in an obviously deplorable state. Frames can, of course, themselves be valuable pieces of furniture, quite apart from the pictures they may happen to surround; indeed, it would not be at all difficult to find examples of frames having an appreciably higher value than the pictures they contain. Ornate, moulded and gilded frames are all vulnerable to damage, sometimes taking knocks that would otherwise have had a sad effect on their canvases. There are techniques available for restoring the patterns of broken decorative plasterwork, then regilding and so forth, but all frames need to be checked for soundness of structure. A frame easing apart at its joints in the corners will obviously be in need of a measure of first-aid.

Before turning the picture back round to start looking at the actual surface of the painting, the plain back of the canvas needs to come in for an alert inspection. The presence of a piece of canvas patching will show where a small-scale repair has formerly been necessary, while any unrepaired tears or splits will be as obvious from the front as they are from the back. Less obvious signs of damage may be indicated by brown stains similar to 'foxing' on paper (see page 125

below). In the case of canvas, these show that there has been a problem with damp during the course of the picture's life, and it could be that a legacy of mould has been left to work away unsuspected underneath the paint, or that the paint and primer are showing signs of bubbling. The feel of the canvas to the touch is also important. If it seems very dry, then you should adopt the technique of placing your ear against the painted surface as you run your finger-tips over the back. A faint 'crackling' sound will tell you that the paint is in the process of lifting away from the canvas and that a complete relining is going to be unavoidable.

Relining means, in fact, that the old canvas has to be entirely dismantled from its stretcher before being remounted on a new piece of canvas by a careful procedure involving bonding with hot wax and ironing. The new canvas is then affixed to a new stretcher. Circumstances in which relining is advisable can include not only paint lifting away from the canvas, but also serious examples of tears or holes, or extensive areas of flaking or cracking. If relining is needed, then this will have to be carried out before any other restoration procedures are put in hand.

The appearance of the front of the painting will also tell you a good deal about its condition, but again it takes practice and experience to make the right interpretations.

(Above, left) Seventeenth-century oval portrait of Lord Paget in armour, attributed to Sir Peter Lely (1618-80). Oil on canvas.

(Above, right) The back of the portrait of Lord Paget by Lely, showing a typical ninteenth-century glue lining on a stretcher.

(Left) Back of a seventeenth-century picture relined in the nineteenth century, showing a Victorian liner's canvas and stretcher. This is typical of the appearance of many English seventeenth and eighteenth-century paintings which have been relined. (Right) Back of an unrestored eighteenth-century painting showing the canvas on its original solid strainer (i.e. without wedges).

You will need to learn to read the signs by using the naked eye as well as invoking the aid of a magnifying-glass.

> Nobody at all interested in the finer technical aspects of old paintings [says Ruhemann] should ever be without the 6 times magnification pocket lens. It is however almost useless unless it is held in the proper way: almost touching one's eyebrow, absolutely parallel with the picture plane and taking care not to cast a shadow on the area being examined ... However, it cannot be stressed too much ... how wrong it is to rush at a picture with magnifying-glasses ... before enjoying and examining it in ordinary light at normal viewing distance.

A maze of craquelure or cracking over the surface, like a pattern of crazy paving, is a natural and even a reassuring feature of any period oil-painting, and it is not in itself anything which needs to cause concern. Nevertheless, the cracking

Back of a typical
nineteenth-century
wedged stretcher in
its original slip and
frame.

Contrast with the
back of a modern
canvas.

demands observant attention if one is to be sure that the paint
is not in fact lifting away. Flaking is a related phenomenon
where flakes of paint have actually been lost and have left
the primer exposed. An oil-painting that has been hung by
its owner too closely above a heat source, such as a radiator,
will often betray this fact by distinct signs of flaking in an
approximate line across the bottom of the canvas.

Hunting Scene, c. 1800, School of George Morland (1763-1804). Badly cracked and in need of restoration.

Badly torn nineteenth-century portrait of a child. Though at first sight in bad condition, restoration is relatively straightforward after relining provided all the canvas is there.

Early eighteenth-century portrait (by Verelst) in the process of restoration – showing old tears and worn patches revealed by cleaning. This is fairly typical of the condition of a picture of this period after brown varnish and old overpainting have been removed.

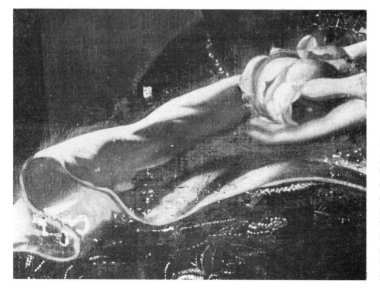

Detail from the Verelst portrait, showing overcleaning. Dark areas are especially vulnerable, light areas are usually more robust. The shadowed area under the hand has been scrubbed almost completely away, whereas the light on the drapery has survived intact.

Extensively flaking ninteenth-century portrait after relining and before retouching.

(Left) Early nineteenth-century landscape on panel showing flaking and areas of paint cupping up and about to flake. The picture cannot be cleaned until the flaking has been treated.

(Below) The same panel in the process of being cleaned. A badly browned varnish is being removed with solvents.

(Top) Eighteenth-century still-life showing obscuring effects of old brown varnish on delicate glazes of grapes and other fruit.

(Above, left) Seventeenth-century portrait of a child, uncleaned since the nineteenth century, showing dramatic effect of removing just the surface dirt. Traces of an old brown varnish can be seen in the cleaned area.

(Above, right) An Edwardian portrait showing airborne dirt in the process of removal (cleaned area top right).

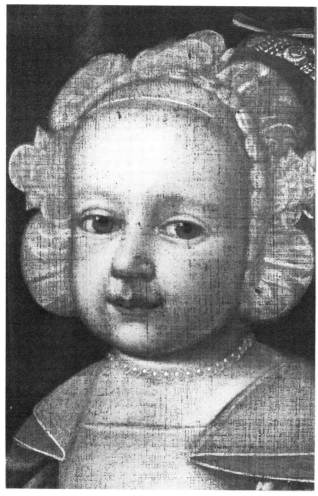

Seventeenth-century portrait of a child showing the paint worn by overzealous cleaning in the nineteenth-century. Damage like this is often overpainted extensively by trade restorers, giving a spurious appearance to the painting. However, if the tiny damages are carefully spotted out individually the picture will retain its authentic quality.

Back of a painting on wood panel showing a cradle to hold together a warped or cracked panel. The horizontal thicker bars are glued to the panel but have bridges to accommodate the upright bars which are not glued but free to move within the constraints of the bridges. The wood panel can thus expand and contract across the grain if its humidity should change. A completely fixed frame would cause the panel to split eventually.

121

It is now that the whole purpose of giving an oil-painting a top surface of varnish becomes clear as you look at the picture itself, inclining its plane against the light to check for dull areas. Where these are present they will show that the varnishing has not been evenly carried out over the whole of the painted area; and if it should have been unevenly done (though this is fairly improbable with the work of a professional as opposed to an amateur artist), then years of dust and the settlement of other atmospheric deposits (nicotine, carbon and goodness knows what other chemical outfalls from different results of human activity) will have attached themselves to the very substance of the paint. The natural consequence of this will be that cleaning the picture becomes a tricky operation since it will be impossible to remove the dirt without also doing damage to the paint and the artist's original brush strokes. And once this has happened, then the paint, too, will need to be restored.

On the other hand, where a reliable layer of varnish has been smoothly applied all over, it will have achieved its protective purpose and provided a barrier against polluting influences by taking the brunt of their assault over the course of the years. For a picture that is otherwise structurally sound, the action then needed to restore it to its handsome original appearance could, at its simplest, be a straightforward surface clean using a mild alkaline wax. This will be enough to remove layers of soot and grime, though fly specks tend to be more tenacious and as a rule need to be flicked off, one by one, with the tip of a small scalpel.

As soon as it is necessary to remove the layer of varnish from an oil-painting, however, then simplicity can never be assumed and the restorer must proceed with great care at every stage. The strength of the solvent the restorer uses is critical: it needs to be strong enough to remove the varnish but not so strong as to remove the paint. It must, moreover, be tested at each stage to make sure the mixture of ingredients is correct for the picture being worked on, since every picture is different in its responses. Old varnishes also react in very different ways from modern varnishes, as do old and modern paints, and so the complexities multiply and drive home the point that this is not a field for the inexperienced to enter at whim.

Paintings done not on canvas but on one of the other types of support available to artists — panels of solid wood (often used for tempera), plywood, hardboard or cardboard — raise a slightly different set of problems when it comes to conservation. A wooden panel, it goes without saying, can be directly vulnerable to attack by woodworm, and here the worm is undermining the very integrity of the painting rather than just its frame or surround. Cardboard can play host to silverfish, those silvery insects which sometimes nest down in and do damage to the spines of books or papers. Levels of atmospheric humidity or dryness may also be factors that have an effect. The dryness in the air typically associated with an efficient central-heating system in a well-insulated house, for instance, can also cause a panel to split or to warp, however mature or well seasoned the wood from which it is made. Warping, in its turn, subjects the layers of paint to unfamiliar stresses and strains that then lead on to serious flaking or surface undulation.

The restorer will deal with the surface of a painting on wood or board in the same way as one done on canvas. The differences all relate to the nature of the support. Where cracks open up in the painting, reflecting splitting in the underlying wood, they will need to be filled with glue, then with putty, and the panel clamped before the cracks can be disguised by overpainting in a way similar to that necessary where a hole or split has been repaired in a canvas.

Any sort of panel that is splitting or warping, however, is likely to be in need of strengthening by a framework of struts glued to the back, this technique being known as 'cradling'. The warping of a board can also be cured by the technique of placing it slightly above a sheet of damp blotting-paper so that it absorbs moisture through the back. Impregnating it with wax resin to seal in the moisture then ensures that it will not warp again. It is usually recommended that an oil done on cardboard should be provided with struts as a matter of course. Paintings on cardboard are also liable to suffer from small bumps, the treatment for which is to scrape away delicately a part of the board at the back, after which the front of the painting should flatten out of its own accord.

By and large, the problems likely to beset any picture executed on a paper support, whether it is a painting, drawing or print, are going to be broadly similar, with the proviso that certain variations of fragility and sensitivity do need to be allowed for. The paper itself should seldom be a problem so long as the artist or printmaker has used a rag- or linen-based paper or other paper of corresponding quality, and so long as the picture has spent its life being sensibly cared for. If an inferior paper has been used, whatever the reason, then the life of the picture itself will inevitably be shortened, simply because it has been done on a support that lacks long-term

THE CARE
AND REPAIR
OF PICTURES
ON PAPER

stability. The paper may become faded or discoloured, for one thing, while the processes of decay can start to take their toll of the paper's fabric within a matter of only a few decades. The reason for this is that mass-produced commercial papers are seldom free of those chemical impurities, including acids, which in the end bring about their decline or actual destruction.

Librarians and archivists, for example, increasingly find themselves having to solve formidable problems in preserving books, newspapers, original manuscripts and notebooks, many not yet a century old, as the woodpulp-based papers from which they were manufactured start to go through various stages of disintegration. The tendency of such papers to break down over the course of the years is rather like a time-bomb effect in slow motion. As a result, the craft of the paper conservator, with his techniques for stablizing the acid content and structure of papers, is becoming as much in demand as that of the picture restorer. There is also, it follows, an increasing overlap of useful knowledge between the two areas of research. But where a picture needs the attention of paper conservation techniques, it will obviously also have to be quite a valuable one if the time and trouble involved is to be justified.

As we have stressed before, even the acid from the natural secretions of the skin of the hands may eventually have a harmful effect on paper, and the actual handling of any unprotected picture should be kept to a minimum. Pictures done on paper, however, are usually mounted before being placed in a glazed frame whose back panel is then sealed off by brown paper or tape. In this way, the picture is given the maximum protection possible from the effects of its environment. A glazed picture which has been kept hanging on its owner's wall for many years with a broken or inadequate seal is likely to show signs of dirt and impurities round the edges, while it may, behind its glass, also be spotted with the minute corpses of thunderbugs, those infuriating little insects which multiply in sultry weather and seem capable of penetrating into the most unlikely corners. Such a picture will be in need of cleaning, remounting and reframing. An ill-done job of framing can also constitute a threat to the well-being of the picture it is intended to protect. If the framer has used below-standard materials for mounting or backing, for instance, then these may well have an acid content which in the end inflicts damage on the painting or print.

There are many well-established techniques and formulas for cleaning and removing grease or damp stains from paintings, drawings, pastels and prints, whatever media they are done in, but all these procedures are of a specialized and delicate nature; and, again, this is most certainly not an area into which the amateur should venture. Prints, for instance, may be impressed on multiple-layer papers, and although most prints can be safely immersed in water solutions, the layers of paper may proceed to come apart and the top layer then have to be remounted on paper or card. Strictly superficial dirt may, it is true, be rubbed off by soft bread pellets, but this is the point where the tampering of the amateur should cease. 'The best teacher of careful manipulations is a varied experience,' says Ralph Mayer, the author of *The Artist's Handbook*, and a varied experience is certainly an essential prerequisite since a comprehensive set of problems and hazards and their solutions would themselves fill a handbook. There are various recommended and readily available formulas for dealing with 'foxing', as the characteristic small reddish rust-brown blotches that sometimes form on paper are known. In fact these stains are caused by species of mould, and the treatment is to immerse the picture alternately in a bleaching agent and an acid solution. It is a process only to be undertaken by someone who is highly practised in the routines involved. Repairing tears or carrying out retouching on pictures on paper are all likewise tasks for the professional restorer and for no one else, however tempting it may look to have a go on a do-it-yourself basis.

The extremely special nature of this branch of picture restoration was highlighted most dramatically after an attack made with a sawn-off shotgun on the great Leonardo cartoon of the Virgin and Child in the National Gallery in London during the summer of 1987. The layer of protective glass in front of this subtle masterwork in chalk and charcoal took the main force of the blast from the shotgun pellets. The damage done to the cartoon itself, affecting an area about six inches square, was nevertheless profound. Minute splinters of glass had been driven into the fabric and this portion of the paper was also greatly fragmented. The restoration in this case involved many months of dedicated and delicate effort, the restorers often working on the fibres and fragments of the paper with tweezers under a microscope. Because the whole stress of conservation at the National Gallery has been on oil-paintings, it was necessary in the face of this crisis to bring in advisers from other institutions such as the British Museum and the Victoria and Albert Museum where the conservation and repair of work on paper is a more familiar preoccupation.

To emphasize the point one last time, it is not the concern of dealers and collectors to do the work of the conservator and restorer. The important thing for these people is to be able to recognize where and when the advice or attention of a specialist is needed to maintain the integrity of a work of art. It is equally important to have a broad knowledge of the hazards and to keep to a minimum the chances of any picture encountering them. In this respect, the need for care and kind treatment cannot be over-stressed.

Many museums today exercise a painstaking control over conditions within their exhibition galleries. Levels of humidity (there should be neither too much nor too little moisture in the atmosphere and it should not go above 70 per cent or below 30 per cent), variations in temperature, intensities of lighting and so forth are all strictly monitored and adjusted. Naturally it is rarely practicable to reproduce museum conditions in a private home, but a modicum of common-sense in the way pictures are hung or stored will normally provide sufficient safeguards.

Taking an exaggerated example first, you would be foolish indeed if you were to hang a nice water-colour in your bathroom for several years and expect it to emerge from its ordeal by steam and condensation in good shape. You should be equally wary of hanging any painting within an area which is subject to the influence of cooking activities, or of placing it close to a source of heat — say, directly above a radiator. Similarly, you would be unwise to hang a picture immediately above an open fireplace whose chimney was persistently inclined to smoke when the wind was in a certain direction. Heat and too much dryness will upset the natural balance of moisture in the paper, and cause seals and defences to shrink and allow dirt and atmospheric impurities to seep behind the frame and get to the picture itself. A wall with a damp problem should not be used for display, as it will encourage mould and insect pests, quite apart from whatever other more direct damage it may cause. On the other hand, if your house has central-heating, you will be well advised to instal an automatic humidifying system, or at least to have radiator hangers.

You should also avoid hanging any picture on an area of wall where direct rays of sunlight strike through a window at any time of the day or year. Even the artificial lighting used in rooms where pictures are hung needs advisedly to be subdued, and lighting from fluorescent tubes is especially damaging because of the large amounts of ultra-violet light they radiate. A special word should, in fact, be said at this point about the general dangers of over-lighting. It has been known for a long while that, to varying degrees, light has an effect on pigments, and that especially delicate and valuable works need to be protected, even sometimes curtained off from the light. The extent to which light also has an effect on the structure of the fabric of paper has, however, only been fully realized in relatively recent times as scientific research has made its study of these effects. The influence of light on paper actually sets in motion a chemical reaction that leads in the first place to brittleness and irreversible deterioration and ultimately to disintegration.

The message is therefore clear: over the long term, keep all lighting as subdued and indirect as it is possible for it to be. Water-colour pigments may be especially vulnerable to the effects of strong light, but even acrylics can be at risk, not because of any threat to their colour stability but because strong light will eventually undermine their support if this happens to be paper. There is thus no room for complacency.

One of the problems the collector can never adequately guard against is where an artist has, for one reason or another, used materials or experimented with media that do not have the virtue of durability. This is not such a cause for concern in the case of works of former times, although, as we saw in an earlier chapter, even the great Sir Joshua Reynolds himself was an arch-offender in this respect. For collectors who do have an interest in more recent art, though — and this applies especially to work done since the 1960s — the matter of durability is one that constantly requires a degree of alertness.

Collages, whether they are flat or three-dimensional, as well as mixed-media compilations with various ingredients, may all contain elements which will not have been chosen with their ability to last a long time especially in mind. Destructive glues and other substances may form part of the structure, and the experimental artist is often more concerned with immediate effects than he is with the idea of his work still being around in fifty years' time. There is, as we suggested in Chapter 1, a certain cult of impermanence in much of twentieth-century art, and nothing lasts for ever in any case. As the American writer Kurt Vonnegut put it in a short piece entitled 'Reflections on My Own Death', 'Anybody with any sense knows that the whole solar system will go up like a celluloid collar by and by.'

From the point of view of the collector this is, of course, all very fine, and many will naturally ask why they should concern themselves with work which places such a low priority on longevity. On the other hand, at least a portion of this lack of staying power may be attributed to ignorance rather than intention, as a result of the notable failure of art schools and colleges to teach basic craftsmanship in picture making and construction during recent years. The schools have, indeed, been known to pour scorn on the very idea that acquiring such crafts could be in any way important.

But all such opinions reflect trends that run more or less in cycles. In due course the pendulum swings back, and we are already seeing a trend towards the reassertion of the value of craftsmanship as a concomitant of effective creativity. Meanwhile, an important sub-group of restorers is increasingly coming into its own: it consists of specialists who set out to deal with problems unique to certain types of modern art.

The dual role of being both buyer and seller implies a need for quick and flexible thinking and generally keeping your wits in trim. It will be clear by now that with pictures, as with antiques and collectables of every kind, the 'feel' for an object becomes a matter of first importance. This is not something that can be taught; it can only be learnt in a practical way through experience. By the 'feel' we mean, of course, the instinct which tells you whether a picture is a good example of the work of an artist whose star is ascending, of whether it is 'right' and untampered with — and also if the frame is original for the painting and matches it in period, or wheth-

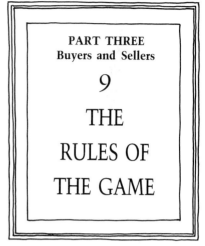

er, despite signs of damage, it may be worth paying a certain sum and adding in the cost of repair before marking up a profit. As we stressed earlier in this book, it can take many months of observation combined with a background measure of scholarship — not to mention a margin for making inevitable errors of judgement — before you can really be confident of developing the canniness that the whole operation requires of you.

This closing chapter is designed to run over the ground one last time, to amplify points already made and to plug any gaps that remain. To this end, returning to the auction- room, we might well take a closer look at the procedures for inspection followed by dealers and ask exactly what a picture tells them when they turn it around to look at the back. Broadly speaking, the objective in looking at the back is to be better informed when it comes to inspecting the front. In the case of a framed picture, such as a water-colour, drawing or print, signs that it has been recently remounted or resealed might lead us to sharpen our suspicions that it could have been tampered with in some way, perhaps to try to touch up or brighten a faded water-colour or even to add a spurious signature to an unsigned work. Such enterprise may be rare but it is not unknown.

With a canvas painting, on the other hand, the information gleaned may be more specific. Where any tears have been repaired, the patching will show up at once, and when we look at the front, we can then observe if the shape of any patch shows through on the surface. If it does, then you may be sure that the job has not been very skilfully carried out and will need to be done again. Where you find that a canvas has been relined, there may have been some serious problems with flaking and paint loss, or it may at some time have been badly torn; hence the surface could show signs of extensive retouching or restoration. And with the class of pictures that mainly concerns us — those most likely to turn up in country sales — the possibility remains that this fact could have a devaluing effect. How the canvas feels to the touch is also important. Where a canvas seems exceptionally dry and brittle, then relining could be necessary; and relining will be essential for any picture that is actually losing its paint. Evidence for former damp damage or mildewing could similarly be made clear by signs on the back and indicate potential sources of trouble, while the presence of woodworm in the frame or other damage by insect pests is also most likely to be detectable from the back.

When a dealer spits on the surface of an old oil-painting and rubs the spit round with his fingers in a circular motion, he is utilizing his saliva to lend a temporary clarification to the varnish and gain a good idea of the original colour tones as these survive under the accumulations of dirt. This, in turn, provides an indicator of the quality of the painting. A dealer may also spit in the signature area to check out the signature of the artist. It will become clear at this point why a magnifying-glass is such an essential tool of the trade. This is the time when it can be used to inspect the craquelure in detail to check that no sections of paint actually seem to be lifting away from the canvas: the cracking should be in the *varnish* rather than in the body of the paint. This is also where a strong light will be helpful to check the evenness of the varnish (an unevenly varnished picture may have absorbed so much dirt as to make cleaning an extremely chancy operation in its unprotected areas) and to see if there are any visible signs of earlier attempts at touching up or restoration. Detecting where a canvas has been 'skimmed' (overcleaned to the extent that the solvents have attacked a layer of paint) is a difficult area for the amateur to become proficient in, and only practice at observing actual cases will build up the growth of confidence — and with it a lessening of the chances of being misled. Certain high-quality reproduction prints of water-colours can deceive the eye into thinking them to be originals at a first or even a second glance. In these cases, a quick check at the edge of the water-colour with the indispensable magnifying-glass will bring out the telltale fine but even patterns of the 'screen', as the matrix used in the printing of illustration work is termed. With water-colours, though, as we have remarked earlier, the chances of coming across a deliberate fake are very slender. One must, of course, always beware of student or enthusiast's copies, but in general common sense will sift these out, and usually such works are done from originals so well known that no intention to deceive was ever present. Good quality copies may also have their value, of course.

The expertise of the auctioneers and their staff certainly helps to some extent to control the number of forgeries arriving on the market, although the general rise in art values equally means that the temptations for the forger increase rather than diminish with time, the work of certain artists moving into a price bracket where making the attempt begins to look rewarding. Everyone involved in the field therefore needs to be constantly on their guard, but, despite the example of Mr Tom Keating and the alternative versions of Samuel Palmer drawings with which he managed to fool the experts, it is no easy venture to produce an entirely convincing fake. To avoid suspicion, the weave of a canvas, for instance, must be of the correct period, as must the style of the frame. This is one reason why we need to tread a little warily wherever an oil-painting is obviously not in its original frame, or where a nineteenth-century drawing turns up in a mount that has a new appearance. And even though the work itself may be entirely authentic, the fact of reframing or remounting can indicate that it has been recently circulating in the trade and so will lack the interest of work that is freshly on the market after having spent many years tucked away in a private collection.

The feeling for the general 'rightness' of a picture, for the way it matches with its frame and style of presentation, is once again an area where the accumulation of experience must count for a great deal. Similarly, the sense of something being 'wrong' somewhere is an instinct that needs to be based on an informed background. These are very much matters that depend on a wealth of observation over time, but, as Robert Wraight said in *The Art Game*: 'The sale-rooms are the best free universities there are for an education in the art game and the knowledge you gain there over the years will be invaluable.'

AUCTIONEERS' CODES AND TERMS OF SALE In the case of Sotheby's and Christie's, the terms and conditions of business with both buyers and sellers are laid down in considerable detail in the small print to be found at the back of all their catalogues. With regional auction houses, the conditions of business are likely to be

(Right) A well-framed picture, late eighteenth century, School of Morland. The frame is of the correct period and no doubt original. The old gilding on the simple sections with crossed ribbons and just the right amount of fancy decoration in the narrow running pattern enhance perfectly the quiet dignity of the scene.

(Above, left) A late eighteenth-century English portrait in an appropriate period frame.

(Above, right) A badly framed picture: a small, understated oil-painting framed in a fussy reproduction pierced gilt frame, more suitable for a mirror. The tranquil simplicity of the scene is not enhanced; the frame is glazed and the gilding brash. The whole effect makes an attractive nineteenth-century oil-painting look like a cheap modern coloured print.

less complex in detail, but the gist will be the same. These conditions broadly speaking constitute a contract, and it is certainly necessary to be aware of the disclaiming elements they contain. The effect of these is to place the onus on the buyer to satisfy himself that the status and condition of the goods he is bidding for are as they are described in the auction catalogue. In other words, the implication is plainly stated: by the act of entering into the bidding, you are confirming that you are in agreement with the auctioneer's description of the item. Almost the only circumstance in which you would be likely to get your money back would be one where you could demonstrate that a certain work turned out on later examination to be a deliberate forgery.

In this context, it is as well to be clear on the significance of auctioneers' coding systems as these are offered in their descriptions. The key to them will be found under the 'Glossary' heading in every auctioneer's catalogue, and here, as you will notice, the phrase 'in our opinion' emerges with striking regularity. That is to say the auctioneer, as agent for the sale between vendor and buyer, disclaims making an absolute statement but expresses an opinion with which you may agree or disagree as you please. Auctioneers and their staff are experienced, skilled and reliable as a rule, but are not above making an occasional mistake. For this reason, it is a healthy practice never to take a description at face value but to regard it with at least a measure of scepticism.

In summarizing a fairly standard glossary of descriptive phrases, we find that the following apply:

(a) If the full forename/s and surname of the artist are given, then, in the opinion of the auctioneers, it is an authentic work by the artist.

(b) If an initial or initials precede the surname, then, in the opinion of the auctioneers, it is a work of the correct period for the artist and may be his work, wholly or in part.

(c) If only a surname is given, it indicates an opinion that here may be a work of the school or by a follower, or by another artist working in his style, the date remaining uncertain.

(d) If 'ascribed to' is stated, then the attribution is traditional.

(e) If 'attributed to' is stated, then a recent but still tentative attribution based on style is indicated.

(f) If the word 'after' appears adjacent to the name of the artist, then this picture will be thought to be a copy, not an original.

(g) The specification 'signed' indicates an opinion that the signature is authentic.

(h) The specification 'dated' indicates an opinion that a date recorded on the painting is authentic.

Different firms of auctioneers will have their own slight variations to play within this general scheme, but the broad principles will always be the same. In this context, it is interesting, however, to take note of the fact that in 1987, according to a report in *The Times* (25 November), a dealer succeeded in prompting a local Trading Standards Department to bring a successful prosecution against an auctioneer under the Trades Descriptions Act for wrongly claiming a painting to be by Thomas Girtin when it was, in fact, by a follower. The action represented an interesting precedent, the practical consequences of which seemed likely to be that auctioneers might not be able to shelter so securely behind their disclaimer clauses in future.

There are several pieces of auctioneer's jargon that you are likely to come across from time to time, so it will be as well to know what they signify:

Against you all: an auctioneer will use this phrase to show he has received from a client unable to attend the sale a bid (known as a 'commission bid') that overtops any of the bids made from the floor of the auction-room.

Bought in: a lot is 'bought in' when the bidding fails to reach a minimum price (known as the 'reserve price') that the owner has set on his property. The auctioneer bids on the owner's behalf if necessary, and in effect 'buys the item in' if it fails to make the figure in question.

Buyer's premium: this is a premium (usually 10 per cent of the purchase price) that some auction houses charge to successful bidders. If you are doing business with an auction house where a buyer's premium applies, then remember to take this into account in your calculations.

In the folio: any unframed water-colours, drawings or prints that are available for viewing in boxes or portfolios are referred to thus by the auctioneer.

Off the wall: an auctioneer may have recourse to the device of taking bids 'off the wall' where he holds a reserve price or a commission bid and there is only one bidder on the floor.

On the hammer: a late bid, made just as the auctioneer is bringing down his hammer, is referred to as being 'on the hammer', and reopening the bidding at this point is a matter for the auctioneer's discretion.

It only remains to re-emphasize that all the small print in your auctioneer's catalogue is important and that you should not neglect to spend the time necessary to make sure you are familiar with whatever it says.

Terms of sale from Sotheby's catalogue.

Important information for buyers and sellers

Catalogues and Price Lists
These can be obtained on Annual Subscription from our Catalogue Subscription Department, 34-35 New Bond Street, London W1A 2AA. Telephone: (01) 493 8080.

Terms of Sale by Auction
VENDORS' COMMISSION
A commission of 10% is payable by the vendor on the hammer price of lots sold for £1,000 or more (15% up to £999), with the exception of the following:
Wine (per consignment) – 10% for lots sold for £500 or more (15% up to £499).

Postage Stamps; Coins, Medals and Militaria; Conduit Street (inclusive of all charges except VAT) – 15% throughout.

Veteran and Vintage Cars (excluding entry fee) – 10% throughout.

Minimum Commission charges may be levied on lower value lots (for full details see property receipts).

VAT
Commission and illustrations are subject to VAT for U.K. residents and those residents of E.E.C. countries who are not registered for VAT.

INSURANCE
The rate of premium payable by the vendor is 1% of the hammer price of both sold and unsold lots and this premium is subject to VAT to both U.K. and foreign vendors.

BUYERS' PREMIUM
A buyers' premium of 10% of the hammer price is payable by the buyers of all lots, together with VAT on such premium. Where indicated by a dagger in the catalogue, VAT is payable on the hammer price.

CONDUIT STREET SALES
Pre-sale advices and catalogues will not be sent to vendors prior to a sale. The date of the sale in which your property is entered, will normally be fixed at the time of agreement for sale. Vendors will receive a copy of the catalogue, settlement cheque and settlement advice one week after the date of sale.

Payment of Sale Proceeds
Payment is made by a Sterling cheque. We are normally happy, however, to make payments (and to quote reserves) in the currency of the vendor's choice. Also, if requested, we will buy currency forward at the rate of exchange prevailing on the next working day after the date of sale.

Order Bids
If instructed we will execute bids and advise intending purchasers. This service is free. Lots will always be bought as cheaply as is allowed by such other bids and reserves as are on our books. Orders, when placed by telephone, are accepted only at the sender's risk and must be confirmed before the sale by letter or telex.

Written Valuations
The provision of written valuations for Insurance, Inheritance Tax (Probate), Sale by Private Treaty, or other purposes, is an important part of Sotheby's service. Valuations can be arranged through any of our International offices or salerooms in London, Billingshurst or Chester.
Valuation fees vary according to the nature and amount of work to be undertaken, but will always be highly competitive. We shall be pleased to refund the valuation fee charged on any item, if it is consigned to us for sale within a reasonably short period of time after the valuation.

Inspections
We will inspect properties and advise owners who wish to sell at auction without charge. In certain instances however it may be necessary to charge out of pocket and travelling expenses.

Export Licences
A licence from the Department of Trade will be required before items of certain kinds may be exported from the United Kingdom. A further licence will also be required for any items made of or incorporating animal material (e.g. ivory, whalebone, tortoiseshell). Applications for both licences can be made by our Shipping Department upon request.

Advice to Bidders
Further advice to bidders and purchasers follows the bidding slip printed after the last lot in this sale.

MAKING THE
BIDS

The auctioneer is very much a maestro in his own domain; some auctioneers, indeed, are virtuosos in the art and visibly enjoy every moment they are able to spend on the podium. But perhaps one of the least obvious things for the newcomer to auctioneering circles to grasp is the way that bids advance as the auction of an item proceeds. The way in which the intervals of the bids move forward is, in fact, at the auctioneer's discretion. He will obviously work to get a starting bid of the sort of magnitude he is looking for, and then, with each successive bid, will advance the price in whatever units he feels to be appropriate to the picture under his hammer. Where the bidding is brisk, he will most probably advance the bids by greater leaps then he would where it is sluggish. In other words, the mechanism is entirely adaptable to the occasion. With a job-lot of undistinguished prints that he wants to clear, the bidding may go at only a pound or two a time. With a work by a well-known artist, the intervals may go in hundreds or even in thousands of pounds, narrowing down as the upper limits of the bidding are reached to test the determination of the rival bidders who remain in the field. The justification for the auctioneer acting in his role remains, after all, to gain the best possible price he can for his client, the vendor.

It is undoubtedly this organic element of never knowing quite how the bidding will end up that gets the adrenalin circulating in the system. The question therefore becomes how do you manage to avoid being carried away in a fit of enthusiasm? The obvious answer is that you stick, in a disciplined way, to the target prices you have marked in your catalogue along the lines suggested in Chapter 2. There may be occasions when this requires some strength of character, but, having said that, it should also be remembered that the market tends all the time to move upwards, even in troubled financial times. And, again, your purpose may be divided. Clearly, if you see a choice item that is going to plug a gap in your personal collection, then you are likely to press on to greater limits to secure it. But either way, you need to have confidence in the prices you set in the first place. Where you find yourself outbid, then either your calculations underrated the possibilities or else your rival had a good reason, with which you could not compete, for stepping up the bidding.

There are, of course, many qualifications and questions that you will have to bear in mind as you come to make your final, possibly split-second decisions. The condition of the painting is one of these, and while there is no need to be

136

put off by dark old varnish or a small tear in a canvas, you do need to give thought to the costs, say, of relining if this looks a likely necessity. At current rates, these can range from approximately £25 for a small canvas of 300 square inches to over £100 for one of 2,250 square inches. Other restoration costs will be comparable, for the skills of restorers are much in demand and their time is naturally expensive. The cost of restoring a 'skimmed' canvas properly could, for instance, run to an amount directly comparable with the picture's value. These are the areas where you may be best advised to leave well alone, though if you insist on proceeding, you certainly need to be clear on those rules of thumb for a profit margin that you should carry in your head at all times.

In the interesting balancing act between the price to pay that will gain you a margin of profit and the price being defined by the direction taken by the bidding, you will need to work out your own system of reckoning. This clearly has to be based on the profit percentage for which you are generally searching. A typical line of reasoning could well run as follows:

PROFIT AND MARK-UP

Last year a comparable picture by the same artist as the one I now have an interest in fetched £450 at auction. Allowing for the continuing appreciation of values, I am therefore prepared to go to £500 in the bidding, knowing that I have a good chance of selling it on for between £650 and £700 to this dealer or that dealer (having a shrewd idea at the back of my mind of what he will in turn charge for it in his showroom).

In other words, in this example you are looking for a mark-up of between 30 and 40 per cent, with 30 per cent as the lower limit. If the bidding now goes to £550, you will have slipped below your minimum percentage margin and should, by that stage, have retired from the contest gracefully. If the picture has an awkward, badly patched tear in the canvas, and you suspect that this could cost you £25 to get properly repaired, you would need to drop your ceiling for bidding from £500 to £475 to bring this additional factor into the reckoning.

The percentage figure for your mark-up, always remember, is not the same as your profit margin. The actual figures for your profits will need to take into account your out-of-pocket costs and expenses. Indeed, you cannot technically be in profit until these have been covered. It will probably be perfectly reasonable at the beginning to fix in your mind the 30 per cent figure for a minimum mark-up. This can then be

(Above) A sale of old masters at Sotheby's on 10 December 1986 in which Rembrandt's *Portrait of a Girl Wearing a Gold-trimmed Cloak* sold for £7,260,000 – an auction record for a painting by Rembrandt.

(Below) On a more modest scale, an auction taking place at Lacy Scott's, Bury St Edmunds, March 1988.

tested out in practice as you form a more detailed impression of how much this adventure is costing you as you pay out the necessary subscriptions and expenses, travel about the countryside and put up at reasonably comfortable hotels on occasion. You may then feel that you really ought to be more ruthless about going for a higher percentage to justify the operation, or else decide that you feel perfectly relaxed about getting a slightly lower figure in the bag. It is entirely for you to decide in line with the scale of your ambitions. If, after a time, you should yourself come to resell anything at auction, then you will, it goes without saying, be looking for a comparable improvement in value once the auctioneer's commission has been taken into account.

Whether you are a collector or a dealer, or both at the same time, the question of how you set about insuring your pictures is an important one. At a time when the advantages of putting money into a fine art collection are frequently demonstrated, and when so much press publicity is given to ascending values in the work of a wide spectrum of artists, then it follows that artworks in general are going to have more and more of an attraction for professional criminals. What is more, thieves are perfectly capable of educating themselves to the point where they can be selective in what they go for: the work that is being sought after and hence that is capable of being quickly disposed of. We are living at a time when the theft of artworks is something of a boom industry. **INSURANCE**

The chances of stolen pictures ever being reunited with their true owners are generally admitted to be remote. It is nothing unusual for pictures and antiques of all kinds, once they have been purloined, to promptly disappear into the shadier areas of the market and leave no trail behind them. If they should resurface some time later, the chances of lesser-known pictures by less famous artists being recognized by someone who knows about their theft is not, on the whole, very likely. It is, in any case, most probable that good-quality work stolen by knowing criminals will have been spirited abroad in a matter of only a few days of being taken. Even star turns among paintings have been known to disappear without trace, or to suffer the fate of a Corot taken from a French museum in 1984 only to emerge in private hands in Tokyo in 1987, its new owner being able to take advantage, after a time lapse of only two years, of the rights of proprietorship applying under Japanese law. Different countries have different laws, and once a work of art has been taken out of the country, the original owner may lose his title purely through technicalities, irrespective of the self-evident justice of his case.

It is not only theft, of course, that has to be insured against. Devastation, damage and loss may be caused by fire or flood, by the burst pipe in the attic the winter weekend you happened to be away, by the faulty piece of electric wiring you did not know was heading for trouble, by the firemen's hoses extinguishing a fire in the room overhead. By and large, where only a few pictures of relatively low value are concerned, the normal household insurance may provide sufficient cover, but as soon as you are dealing with pictures on a more ambitious scale, then your requirements are bound to become more complex and may well lead you into the more specialized field of fine arts insurance and the need for expert advice that this implies.

Insurance hinges on value, and if you have a collection of old masters whose value runs to many thousands or millions of pounds, then the insurance premiums you will be asked to pay are likewise going to be astronomical — if you decide to insure them at all. Certain collectors and private museums have decided to go for the option of living with the risk, but with a modest collection the level of premiums should remain within reach of your pocket. It is obviously sensible to make sure you are adequately covered, and if you are involved with dealing at the same time as you are building up a collection, then you will have two quite distinct requirements: (a) to cover the pictures incorporated into your personal collection at home and (b) to cover those pictures that are temporarily in your ownership while you seek a buyer for them.

Insurance companies are naturally increasingly security conscious nowadays, and you will probably be required to answer a range of questions describing the premises where you keep your pictures, how often these premises are left unoccupied, the types of locks on the doors and windows, whether there is a burglar-alarm system in operation, whether people other than members of your immediate family have access. The circumstances for policies to cover either a permanent collection or goods in short-term owner-ship are broadly similar where the basic policy is concerned, but in the case of a 'business risk' proposal, a supplementary form may seek the answers to a comprehensive set of ques-tions about the way you organize your stocktaking, storage and accounting.

An original picture is, by definition, irreplaceable. How

is an insurance figure therefore to be formulated, since the objective of insurance is to cover the 'replacement' value? The usual way round this difficulty is to arrive at an 'agreed value', meaning a value intended to provide compensation in the event of total loss or to cover repair costs for any damage suffered. With a personal collection of artworks, this figure should be relatively easy to settle, given the proviso that it will need to be reviewed from time to time to take account of new items added to the collection as well as the general upward trend in prices for anything that has been worth collecting in the first place. The figure or figures will obviously be less easy to clarify in circumstances where work is continually passing through your hands and you hold a variable quantity of stock.

The value to apply in the case of a 'business risks' proposal is usually worked out on the basis of averages over a year of business activity. That is to say, the insurer will accept the average value of holdings of stock on a monthly basis for the previous year as these can be supported by your business records. For cover away from the premises (for goods in transit), an estimated daily average value will be sought, with information on the maximum and minimum value, frequency of carryings, estimated average value for pictures out with restorers and so forth. On this basis, however, you will need to have been in business a year before you are able to come up with a set of supporting figures for valuation. At the outset, you will therefore have to agree on a set of notional figures with the insurers after discussing them with their agent. It should not be difficult to arrive at realistic valuations for these in the early stages while you are still finding your way.

Take care to be fully aware of all the terms and conditions included in any policy. It is highly likely, for instance, that there will be a clause excluding cover for theft from an unattended vehicle. This, in turn, can only place the onus on you to be especially security minded. It is also, of course, important for you to double-check that your normal vehicle insurance covers you for business as well as for domestic use.

It might seem from all of this that the insurance angle is fraught with several awkward corners. In the nature of things, the complexities are bound to be there, but at the end of the day, having sought the advice of a company with expertise in the insuring of works of art, you will have in your hands a policy tailored closely to your individual circumstances.

KEEPING THE
BOOKS

Being meticulous over the way you maintain your records of purchases and sales is a good habit to cultivate from the beginning, however informal and modest those beginnings may be. The card-index system suggested earlier will help to impose order in this respect, and will act as your memory bank, each card containing details of the price you paid and the price you obtained as part of its data. Recording this information as a matter of routine will ease your task when you eventually come to prepare your accounts, or pass the information to an accountant for him to prepare them on your behalf.

Once you have started dealing, you are in the position of any other self-employed or freelance operator, your profits (or net income) being income that in due course needs to be declared to the Inland Revenue. Therefore it is important to preserve the notes of sale relating to your purchases as well as to issue invoices or receipts to client dealers who buy from you. These papers will constitute your essential records. You should also keep a careful note of all your expenditure (postages, telephone calls, travel by public transport) together with any receipts (for restaurants and hotels, work done by restorers, materials, stationery and so on) and a record of the mileage you travel in your own car. The cost of travelling in your car, after all, includes a proportion of its maintenance and depreciation costs on top of whatever you may pay out for petrol; and so an agreed mileage allowance of so much a mile is usually deductable from gross income (income before profit). Your subscriptions to trade associations and magazines and related book purchases, as well as the premiums to insure your stock, should all be deductable from your gross profit figures, and hence it is very much in your own interests to keep your records in as much detail as possible, with a full complement of proofs of expenditure.

You may find it is convenient as well to open a separate bank account for your art dealings, to ensure these avoid becoming mixed up with domestic and other matters. This will also be useful for clarification when it comes to including details on your tax return for the first time, at which stage you will be able to specify your own twelve-month financial accounting period to apply throughout the years you continue in business.

COUNTRY-
HOUSE SALES

The 'provenance' of a picture, meaning the source it comes from, is always a matter of interest. For one thing, it represents a detail from the picture's 'biography', and for another, to know that a picture has spent the past fifty years in a named collection is a reassuring indicator of its authenticity. Auctioneers' catalogues vary, however, in the amount of such information they contain, and you may need to make inquiries if you wish to know where a particular picture has originated. Sometimes the vendor may have a reason for wishing to remain anonymous, and it is as well always to remember that a proportion of material on sale at the average auction is being recycled within the trade by dealers who are thinning out their stocks or seeking to raise a bit of cash in hand. This is not the sort of doubt and uncertainty that arises at the country-house auction, an institution that has its own excitements and diversions and deserves a special mention before we are through.

The country-house sale is held at the country seat or manor-house of its distinguished owner, who has, for whatever reason, decided to sell off all or part of the family art collection. Other considerations on one side, viewing days (usually on the two to three days before the auction) give a chance for the merely curious as much as the genuinely interested to tramp through the house free of charge and inspect the interior with its treasures still *in situ*. The collection will have been gathered together over many decades, reflecting idiosyncracies as well as the changes of taste that are bound to occur in any historical period. It will thus consist of works and items of perhaps a highly variable quality and will doubtless contain pleasures and surprises. The day of the auction itself will have about it the air of a grand social occasion, with a marquee perhaps on the lawns and a broadly mixed, impressive gathering of interested parties.

There is general agreement in the trade that country-house sales are among the most wholly enjoyable of events in the seasonal calendar. There is also general agreement that they can be among the most unpredictable since the prices fetched may, from a dealer's viewpoint, begin to look ridiculous. This is because these events do attract the attention of a far wider group of people than those who habitually attend auctions; that is to say, they invariably attract a far higher proportion of 'amateur' bidders who do not have to keep in mind the kind of constraints that the 'professional' dealer needs to observe, and who usually have no idea that such constraints exist. The enthusiasm it is possible to generate as a result of this, on top of the 'everything in the catalogue must go' atmosphere, can easily lead on to the phenomenon known as 'country-house fever', when bids keep travelling indiscriminately above the limits of what are normally thought of as market prices. There may be personal or sentimental motives behind the

A country-house sale. Mentmore Towers, near Leighton Buzzard, Buckinghamshire, former home of the Earl of Rosebery, was offered to the Nation with its contents for a bargain price of £1 million – an offer that was rejected. The sale of the century took place in May 1977 and lasted for ten days. It was hoped that the sale, including works of art and valuable treasures, would realize enough to pay off £4½ million in death duties. In fact, the sale realized £6.6 million.

(Left) Coaches, parasols and marquees provide a fairground atmosphere.
(Right) The auction in progress inside the main marquee.

bids of some, while others may simply be keen not to be left out of the fun or want to be sure of taking something home with them at the close of the day.

Thus, while the 'professional' dealer may wring his hands in despair at some of the antics he sees in progress, the distinguished owner and his auctioneers will be highly pleased with the results of the sale, knowing that over all they could hardly have hoped to do better. Provided therefore that you are willing to take the eccentricities of the country-house auction in your stride, there is no reason why you should not attend one when the chance arises. The advertisements for them appear in the art and antiques trade press with regularity. You will certainly have a guarantee of a congenial day out, and you may pick up something interesting enough in the general *mêlée* to justify making the trip.

DEALINGS
WITH
CLIENTS

It only remains now to consider some of the finer points of your relationships with your clientele and the ways you will build these up as you proceed. The basic advice here is that the more efficient and professional you can appear to be the better. Your style, as we said early on, is for you to decide on, and it may be that you will go for smart typographical designs for your letter-heads and invoice forms or, alternatively, that you will set about things far less formally and use the duplicate books bought from stationers to write out your accounts or receipts.

On the other hand, as we also suggested before, in these days of readily available computers and word-processors, usually of excellent quality and reasonably priced, it seems worth undertaking some research into the equipment and system that would best suit your needs and putting the time on one side to master it. This will give you a freedom to work out your own standard layouts for letters and documents. It will also, in the case of an electronic card-index system, give you speedy access to the most complex data you care to store there.

The main advantage of a word-processor is that it imposes a basic efficiency on the way material is dealt with, utilized and organized, but computers are not everyone's cup of tea and the important thing is to be briskly reliable in the way you handle your paperwork, however you decide to cope with it. This will reflect favourably on your ability to do what you are setting out to do and help you to build your clientele among the dealers. Money is often felt to be a delicate area, and the question then arises of whether you should ever advance credit. The general advice is no, you should not, but ought always to keep your transactions on a cash basis. Throughout the trade, this is a perfectly usual way of doing business and no one is going to take offence because you insist on it. Having made this point, however, it might be that you encounter a situation where making a sale could depend on advancing short-term credit to your buyer. In this eventuality, it has to be very much a matter for your own discretion, but you should never do so without asking for a banker's reference.

More than anything else, it is your gregariousness that will create the possibilities where doors open and useful contacts and leads accumulate. These contacts will not be exclusively among the dealers, but will also come to include individual collectors of whose interests you are aware. Scanning the personal columns in the trade publications, and responding where it is appropriate, will give you additional useful entries for your address-book, and you may also consider using advertising on occasion where you hold an item or items in stock that you know will have a special interest once their existence is made known to the right person. On the more personal level, your address-book will be invaluable for providing you with a basis for putting out mailings of your own price lists when you eventually reach a position where it is possible for you to do so.

In considering the future, the trade itself displays a mixture of optimism and pessimism. As the 1980s advance on the 1990s, the art market has shown itself to be capable of broadly maintaining its buoyancy in the face of international upheavals in currency exchange rates and valuations of stocks and shares. Those who have put some of their money into pictures over the past few years have reason to be at least quietly pleased with the way the market value has sustained itself, and the prospect offered by art is, after all, infinitely more attractive, civilized and satisfying than the jungle on the floor of the stockmarket.

This market buoyancy, on the other hand, makes it inevitable from another viewpoint that good pictures will continue to grow more expensive. It seems clear that the prices for pictures of quality will rise at a faster pace than those for second-rate work. The factor of a scarcity value influencing increases in prices also comes into play here, for, it is said, those who deal in pictures are dealing in a continually diminishing market. The questions arise of how many attics still conceal hidden surprises and how many manor-houses still have treasures to disgorge. Similar fears have often been expressed in the past, but it is also true that in recent years in particular the British antiques and fine arts trade has been responsible for shipping container loads of goods abroad — to the United States and Germany among other countries — on a scale that is quite without precedent, and some would call downright irresponsible.

Yet while we should not be lulled into thinking that the art market is an infinitely renewable resource, somehow the emphasis of what is being sought after mysteriously shifts and changes, the collections are lovingly formed and later dispersed through fate or circumstance. In the long run, trends, in taste as well as in styles of painting, turn back to where they began. It may be that the currents of change are now describing a broader sweep along international rather than strictly national lines, that we will have to adjust our ideas about preserving a local heritage and that, in the end, we shall all stand to be the cultural beneficiaries. It simply does not seem in any way realistic to imagine a time when the colourful world of auctioneers and dealers will enter into extinction.

SELECTED READING LIST

Behrman, S.N., *Duveen*, Hamish Hamilton, London, 1952; reissued by André Deutsch, London, 1986. A thoroughly entertaining biography of the grandest dealer of them all.

Gimpel, René, *Diary of an Art Dealer*, translated from the French by John Rosenberg, with an Introduction by Sir Herbert Read, Hamish Hamilton, London, 1986. Gimpel's diary is a warm and human document that throws a good deal of light on the art trade between the wars.

Hermann, Frank, *Sotheby's: Portrait of an Auction House*, Chatto & Windus, London, 1980. A standard and excellent history of a leading auction house.

Rheims, Maurice, *The Glorious Obsession*, Souvenir Press, London, 1980. The autobiographical reminiscences of a leading French auctioneer.

Taylor, John Russell, and Brooke, J., *The Art Dealers*, Hodder & Stoughton, London, 1969. Still a cogent account of the interacting intricacies between artists, dealers and market forces, among other related topics.

Wraight, Robert, *The Art Game*, Leslie Frewin, London, 1965; revised edition under the title of *The Art Game Again*, Leslie Frewin. London, 1974. This splendidly sceptical and trenchant book is still good value for reading.

AUCTIONEERS AND DEALERS

Gombrich, E.H., *Art and Illusion*, Phaidon, 1960. A source book on the philosophy of art by one of the leading art historians of our time. (Gombrich is also the author of the valuable *The Story of Art*, 1972.)

Janson, H.W., *History of Art*, third edition, Thames & Hudson, London, 1987. Comprehensive and scholarly.

THE HISTORICAL AND TECHNICAL BACKGROUND

Mallalieu, H.L., *Understanding Watercolours*, Antique Collectors' Club, Woodbridge, 1984. A useful survey of the methods and styles of the English water-colourists.

Mayer, Ralph, edited by Edwin Smith, *The Artist's Handbook of Material and Techniques*, Faber & Faber, London, 1951; revised edition, Faber & Faber, London, 1964. A comprehensive guide to the technicalities and practicalities behind the production of art of every kind.

Osborne, Harold (ed.), *The Oxford Companion to Art*, Oxford University Press, 1970. Richly informative in the best tradition of the Oxford Companion volumes.

Pevsner, Nikolaus, *The Englishness of English Art*, Architectural Press, London, 1956. A percipient exploration of the trends and character of art in England.

Spalding, Frances, *British Art Since 1900*, Thames & Hudson, London, 1986. A critical and up-to-date history of British artists in the present century.

CARE, RESTORING AND FRAMING

Aldridge, Tim, *Restoring Oil Paintings: a Practical Guide*, Bishopsgate Press, London, 1984. A basic guide for those who wish to explore the techniques of restoration, with the caveat that they should practise only on pictures of no value.

Burns, J.T., *Framing Pictures*, Herbert Press, London, 1978. A good introductory handbook for those who wish to attempt their own mounting and framing.

Keck, Caroline K., *How to Take Care of Your Paintings*, Scribners, New York, 1978. A book of basic advice on caring for a picture collection.

Ruhemann, Helmut, *The Cleaning of Paintings: Problems and Potentialities*, Faber & Faber, London, 1968. Usually and justifiably regarded as the picture restorer's 'bible'.

Walden, Sarah, *The Ravished Image, or How to Ruin Masterpieces by Restoration*, with a Foreword by Sir Ernest Gombrich, Weidenfeld & Nicolson, London, 1985. A counter-perspective on the trend towards restoring paintings at all costs.

MINIATURES

Foscett, Daphne, *British Portrait Miniatures*, Hamlyn, London, 1968. An excellent introductory history to the British miniature tradition.

Churchill, W.A., *Watermarks in Paper in Holland, England, France, etc. in the XVII and XVIII centuries and their interconnection*, M. Hertzberger & Co., Amsterdam, 1935. The standard work on the history and identification of watermarks.

Hunter, Dard, *Papermaking*, Cresset, 1957. The standard book on the subject by its leading historian.

Beynton-Williams, Roger, *Investing in Maps*, Transworld Publishers, London, 1971. An indispensable volume for any collector who intends to concentrate on this field.

Gascoigne, Bamber, *How to Identify Prints: A Complete Guide to Manual and Mechanical Processes from Woodcut to Ink Jet*, Thames & Hudson, London, 1987. Both a manual on all the print-making processes and a guide to their identification.

Hodgkiss, A.G., *Discovering Antique Maps*, Shire Publications, Princes Risborough, 1981. A concise introductory text to a specialist area.

Mackenzie, Ian, *British Prints: Dictionary and Price Guide*, Antique Collectors' Club, Woodbridge, 1987. A book that will certainly be needed by anyone who intends to go in for prints.

Simmons, Rosemary, *Collecting Original Prints*, Quiller Press in association with Christie's Contemporary Art, London, 1980. An admirable guide for the beginner and the more experienced print collector.

Russell, Ronald, *Discovering Antique Prints*, Shire Publications, 1982. A concise introductory guide to the complexities of this field.

Keating, Tom, with Frank and Geraldine Norman, *The Fake's Progress*, Hutchinson, London, 1977. The engaging autobiography of a forger who became a folk hero for the way he fooled the experts.

Schüller, Sepp, *Forgers, Dealers, Experts: Adventures in the Twilight Art of Forgery*, translated from the German by James Cleugh, Arthur Barker, London, 1960. A history of classic exploits in forgery, including those of Han van Meegeren.

PAPER

PRINTS
AND
MAPS

FORGERS

Appendix I
Auction Houses
in Great Britain Listed by Towns

The publishers would be grateful to receive details of any changes to the information listed.

The auction houses listed here either hold regular auctions devoted to works of art or else feature pictures among their specialities of interest. Many other auctions of mixed sales are held up and down the country during the season, and these may well include interesting pictures from time to time. Sales of estates or house contents, sometimes conducted on the premises concerned, can, of course, similarly throw up work that is worthy of consideration. It is essential to keep an eye on the specifications listed in notices of auction sales both in the local press and in such specialist publications as the *Antiques Trade Gazette*, as well as on the calendar of auctions given in *Antiques Collecting*.

London:
Bonhams, Montpelier Gardens,
Montpelier Street, Knightsbridge,
London SW7 1HH
tel. (01) 584 9161

Bonhams Chelsea, 65-69 Lots Road,
King's Road, London SW10 0RN
tel. (01) 351 1380

Borough Auctions, 6-8 Park Street, Borough
Market, London SE1
tel. (01) 407 9577

Christie's 8 King Street, St James's, London
SW1Y 6QT
tel. (01) 839 9060

Christie's South Kensington,
85 Old Brompton Road,
London SW7 3JS
tel. (01) 581 7611

Highgate Auctions, Warehouse No. 8,
Camden Goods Depot, Chalk Farm Road,
London NW1 2RL
tel. (01) 267 2124

Phillips Blenstock House, 7 Blenheim Street,
New Bond Street, London W1Y 0AS
tel. (01) 629 6602

Phillips West 2, 10 Salem Road, London
W2 4BU
tel. (01) 221 5303

Phillips Marylebone, Hayes Place,
Lisson Grove, London NW1 6UA
tel. (01) 723 2647

Rosebery's (incorporating Harvey's Auctions
Ltd), 3-4 Hardwick Street, London EC1R 4RB
tel. (01) 837 3418

Sotheby's, 34-35 New Bond Street,
London W1A 2AA
tel. (01) 493 8080

Sotheby's Belgravia, 19 Motcombe
Street, London SW1X 8LB
tel. (01) 235 4311

Aberdeen:
John Milne, 9-11 North Silver Street,
Aberdeen, Grampian AB1 1RJ
tel. (0224) 639336

Ambleside:
Alfred Mossop & Co., Loughrigg Villa, Kelsick
Road, Ambleside,
Cumbria LA22 0BZ
tel. (0966) 33015

Ascot:
Chancellors Hollingsworths, 31 High Street,
Ascot, Berkshire SL5 7HG
tel. (0990) 27101

Axbridge:
Nuttall, Richards & Co., The Town Hall, The
Square, Axbridge, Somerset BS26 2AR
tel. (0934) 732969

Aylsham:
G.A. Key, 8 Market Place, Aylsham,
Norfolk NR11 6EH
tel. (0263) 733195

Banbury:
Buckell & Ballard, 49 Parsons Street, Banbury,
Oxfordshire OX16 8PF
tel. (0295) 53197/8

Bath:
Aldridges — The Auction Galleries, 130-132
Walcot Street, Bath, Avon BA1 5BG
tel. (0225) 62830 and 62839

Phillips Auctioneers – Bath,
1 Old King Street, Bath, Avon BA1 1DD
tel. (0225) 310609 and 310709

Battle:
Burstow & Hewett, Abbey Auction
Galleries and Granary Sale Rooms,
Battle, East Sussex TN33 0AT
tel. (04246) 2374

Billingshurst:
Sotheby's in Sussex,
Billingshurst RH14 9AD
tel. (040381) 3933

Birkenhead:
Robert I. Heyes & Associates, 9 Hamilton
Street, Birkenhead, Merseyside L41 6DL
tel. (051 647) 9104/5

Birmingham:
Biddle & Webb, Icknield Square,
Ladywood Middleway,
Birmingham B16 0PP
tel. (021 455) 8042

Bishop's Stortford:
G.E. Sworder & Sons, Chequers, 19 North
Street, Bishop's Stortford,
Hertfordshire CM23 2LF
tel. (0279) 52441

Bletchingley:
F.G. Lawrence, Norfolk House, 80 High Street,
Bletchingley, Surrey RH1 4PA
tel. (0883) 843323

Bournemouth:
House & Son, Lansdowne House,
Christchurch Road,
Bournemouth, Dorset BH1 3JW
tel. (0202) 26232

Riddetts of Bournemouth, 26 Richmond Hill,
The Square,
Bournemouth, Dorset BH2 6EJ
tel. (0202) 25686

Bradford:
John H. Raby & Son, Salem Auction Rooms,
21 St Mary's Road, Bradford, West Yorkshire
BD8 7QL
tel. (0274) 491121

Bridgnorth:
Perry & Phillips, Newmarket Salerooms,
Newmarket Buildings, Listley Street,
Bridgnorth, Shropshire WV16 4AW
tel. (074 62) 2248

Brigg:
Dickinson, Davy & Markham,
New Salesroom, Elwes Street, Brigg,
South Humberside DN20 8JH
tel. (0652) 53666

Bristol:
Osmond, Tricks & Son, Regent Street Auction
Rooms, Clifton, Bristol, Avon BS8 4HG
tel. (0272) 737201

Bury St Edmunds:
Lacy Scott & Sons, 10 Risbygate Street, Bury
St Edmunds, Suffolk IP33 3AA
tel. (0284) 763531

Cambridge:
Cheffins, Grain and Chalk, The Cambridge
Salesroom, 2 Clifton Road,
Cambridge CB1 4BW
tel. (0223) 358721

Carlisle:
Thomson, Roddick & Laurie, 24 Lowther
Street, Carlisle, Cumbria
tel. (0228) 28939/39636

Cheltenham:
Mallams, 26 Grosvenor Street,
Cheltenham, Gloucestershire GL50 1HZ
tel. (0242) 35712

Chester:
Phillips in Chester, New House,
150 Christleton Road, Chester CH3 5TD,
tel. (0244) 313936

Sotheby's, Booth Mansion,
28-30 Watergate Street, Chester,
Cheshire CH1 2NA
tel. (0244) 315531

Chichester:
Stride & Son, Southdown House, St John's
Street,
Chichester, West Sussex PO19 1XQ
tel. (0243) 782626

Prudential Property Services,
Baffins Hall, Baffins Lane, Chichester, West
Sussex PO1 91VA
tel. (0243) 787548

Wyatt and Son,
59 East Street,
Chichester PO19 1HN
tel. (0243) 786581

Chipping Campden:
Jackson-Stops & Staff, Market House, High
Street, Chipping Campden,
Gloucestershire GL55 6AJ
tel. (0386) 840224

Cirencester:
Moore, Allen & Innocent, 33 Castle Street,
Cirencester,
Gloucestershire GL7 1QD
tel. (0285) 61831

Clevedon:
Hoddell Pritchard, Sixways, Clevedon, Avon
BS21 7NT
tel. (0272) 876699

Crewkerne:
Lawrence Fine Art of Crewkerne,
South Street, Crewkerne, Somerset TA18 8AB
tel. (0460) 73041

Cromer:
Hanbury Williams, 34 Church Street, Cromer,
Norfolk NR27 9OS
tel. (0263) 513247

Dartford:
Albert Andrews (Auctions & Sales),
Maiden Lane, Crayford, Dartford, Kent DA1
4LX
tel. (0322) 528868

Diss:
Glennie, Middleton and Bullock,
3 Church Street, Diss, Norfolk IP22 3DD
tel. (0379) 51617

Dorchester:
Hy. Duke & Son, Fine Art Salerooms,
Weymouth Avenue, Dorchester, Dorset DT1
1DG
tel. (0305) 65080

Dorking:
P.F. Windibank, 18-20 Reigate Road, Dorking,
Surrey
tel. (0306) 884556

Eastbourne:
Edgar Horn, 49-50 South Street,
Eastbourne, East Sussex BN21 4XB
tel. (0323) 22801/3

Edgbaston:
Biddle & Webb, Enfield Hall, Islington Row,
Edgbaston,
Birmingham B165 1QA
tel. (021 643) 4380

Fellows & Sons, Bedford House,
88 Hagley Road, Edgbaston, Birmingham B16
8LU
tel. (021 454) 1261/1219

Edinburgh:
Phillips in Scotland, 65 George Street,
Edinburgh, Lothian EH2 2JL
tel. (031 225) 2266

Ely:
George Comins & Son, 3 Chequer Lane,
Ely, Cambridgeshire CB7 4NT
tel. (0353) 2256

Exeter:
Phillips, Alphin Brook Road,
Alphington, Exeter, Devon EX2 8TH
tel. (0392) 39025/6

Fakenham:
Long & Beck, 2 Oak Street, Fakenham,
Norfolk NR21 9EB
tel. (0328) 2231

Fareham:
Austin & Wyatt, 79 High Street,
Fareham, Hampshire PO16 7AX
tel. (0329) 234211/4

Folkestone:
Phillips, 11 Bayle Parade,
Folkestone, Kent CT20 1SQ
tel. (0303) 45555

Frome:
Cooper & Tanner, 14 North Parade, Frome,
Somerset BA11 1AU
tel. (0373) 62045

Glasgow:
Christie's in Scotland,
164-166 Bath Street,
Glasgow, Strathclyde G2 4TC
tel. (041 332) 8134/7

Phillips in Scotland,
207 Bath Street, Glasgow G23 3DG
tel. (041 221) 8377

Glastonbury:
Cooper & Tanner, 41 High Street,
Glastonbury, Somerset BA6 9DS
tel. (0458) 31077

Gloucester:
Bruton, Knowles & Co., Albion Chambers,
111 Eastgate, Gloucester,
Gloucestershire GL1 1PZ
tel. (0452) 21267

Godalming:
Messenger, May, Baverstock, 93 High Street,
Godalming, Surrey GU7 1AL
tel. (048 68) 23567

Gorlston-on-Sea:
Hilham's, 53 Springfield Road and 44 Baker
Street, Gorlston-on-Sea,
Norfolk NR31 6AD
tel. (0493) 62152

Grantham:
William H. Brown, Westgate Hall,
Grantham, Lincolnshire NG31 6QF
tel. (0476) 68861/3

Harrogate:
Morphets, 4-6 Albert Street, Harrogate, North
Yorkshire HG1 1JL
tel. (0423) 502282/5

Black Horse Agencies –

Renton & Renton, 16 Albert Street, Harrogate,
North Yorkshire
tel. (0423) 61531

Sotheby, 8-12 Montpelier Parade,
Harrogate, North Yorkshire HG1 2TJ
tel. (0423) 501466/7

Hartlepool:
Norman Hope & Partners, 2 South Road,
Hartlepool,
Cleveland TS24 7SG
tel. (0429) 267828

Haverhill:
Boardman, Fine Art Auctioneers, Station Road
Corner,
Haverhill, Suffolk, CB9 0EY
tel. (0440) 3784

Haywards Heath:
T. Banister & Co., Market Square, Haywards
Heath, Sussex RH16 1DH
tel. (0444) 412402

Hereford:
Stooke, Hill & Co., (incorp. Duncan Heins),
24 Widemarsh Street, Hereford, Hereford and
Worcester
tel. (0432) 272413

Honiton:
Taylor's, Honiton Galleries,
205 High Street, Honiton, Devon EX14 8LF
tel. (0404) 2404

Horsham:
Garth Denham & Associates, Horsham Auction Galleries,
31 The Carfax, Horsham, West Sussex
tel. (0403) 53837

Hove:
Graves, Son & Pilcher, 71 Church Road, Hove,
Sussex BN3 2GL
tel. (0273) 735266

Huddersfield:
Eddisons, 4-6 High Street, Huddersfield, West
Yorkshire HD1 2LS
tel. (0484) 33151

Huntingdon:
The Prudential Fine Art Auctioneers, The
Salerooms, St Ives, Huntingdon,
Cambridgeshire PE18 6PQ
tel. (0480) 68144

Ilkley:
Dacre, Son & Hartley, 1-5 The Grove, Ilkley,
West Yorkshire LS29 9HS
tel. (0943) 600655

Ipswich:
Phillips, Dover House, Wolsey Street,
Ipswich, Suffolk IP1 1UD
tel. (0473) 55137

Kidderminster:
Phipps & Pritchard, Bank Buildings,
Kidderminster, Hereford and Worcester DY10
1BU
tel. (0562) 2244/6 and 2187

Kingsclere:
Hants and Berks Auctions, 40 George Street,
Kingsclere, Hampshire
tel. (0635) 298001

Kingston-upon-Thames:
Bonsor Penningtons, Warwick Lodge, 82 Eden
Street,
Kingston-upon-Thames KT1 1DF
tel. (01) 546 0022

Kirkby Lonsdale:
James Thompson, 64 Main Street, Kirkby
Lonsdale, Cumbria LA6 2AJ
tel. (0468) 71555

Knowle:
Phillips Midlands, The Old House, Station
Road, Knowle, Solihull, West Midlands B93
0HT
tel. (056 45) 6151

Knutsford:
Frank R. Marshall & Co.,
Marshall House, Church Hill, Knutsford,
Cheshire WA1 6DH
tel. (0565) 53284

Leamington Spa:
Locke & England, 1 and 2 Euston Place,
Leamington Spa, Warwickshire CV32 4LW
tel. (0926) 27988

Leeds:
Phillips at Hepper House, 17a East
Parade, Leeds, West Yorkshire LS1 2BU
tel. (0532) 448011

Leicester:
Warners, William H. Brown, The Warner Auction Rooms, 16/18 Halford Street, Leicester
LE1 1JB
tel. (0533) 519777

Leigh-on-Sea:
John Stacey & Sons,
Leigh Auction Rooms,
86-90 Pall Mall, Leigh-on-Sea, Essex SS9 1RG
tel. (0702) 77051

Leominster:
Russell, Baldwin & Bright, The Fine Art Sale-
room, Rylands Road, Leominster, Hereford
and Worcester HR6 8JG
tel. (0568) 3897

Lewes:
Clifford Dann Auction Galleries, 20-21 High
Street, Lewes, East Sussex BN7 2LN
tel. (0273) 77022

Gorringe's Auction Galleries, 15 North
Street, Lewes, East Sussex
tel. (0273) 472503

Leytonstone:
Forrest & Co., 79-85 Cobbold Road,
Leytonstone, London E11 3NS
tel. (01) 534 2931

Lichfield:
Wintertons, St Mary's Chambers,
Lichfield, Staffordshire WS13 6LQ
tel. (054 32) 23256

Liverpool:
Outhwaite & Litherland, Kingsway Galleries,
Fontenoy Street, Liverpool,
Merseyside L3 2BE
tel. (051 236) 6561/3

Lowestoft:
Charles Hawkins, Notleys Salerooms, Royal
Thoroughfare, Lowestoft, Suffolk
tel. (0502) 2024/5

Lymington:
Elliott & Green, Auction Salerooms,
Emsworth Row, Lymington,
Hampshire SO4 92E
tel. (0590) 77225

Manchester:
Capes, Dunn & Co., The Auction
Galleries, 38 Charles Street, Manchester M1
7DB
tel. (061 273) 6060

Reeds Rains Prudential, Trinity House,
114 Northenden Road,
Manchester M33 3HD
tel. (061 962) 9237

Mold:
Dodds Property World, Victoria Auction Galleries, Mold, Clwyd CH17 1EB
tel. (0352) 2552

Nantwich:
Peter Wilson & Company, Fine Arts Department, Victoria Gallery,
Market Street, Nantwich, Cheshire CW5 5RL
tel. (0270) 63878/9

Newark:
Richard Watkinson & Son, 17 Northgate,
Newark, Nottinghamshire NG24 1EX
tel. (0636) 77154/77154

Newbury:
Dreweatt – Neate,
Donnington Priory,
Donnington, Newbury, Berkshire RG13 2JE
tel. (0635) 31234

Northampton:
R.L. Lowery & Partners,
Woolpack House, 24 Bridge Street,
Northampton, Northamptonshire NN1 1NT
tel. (0604) 21561

Heathcote Ball & Co., Albion Auction Rooms,
Commercial Street,
Northampton, Northamptonshire NN1 1PJ
tel. (0604) 37263/4

Norwich:
James — Norwich Auctions,
33 Timberhill, Norwich,
Norfolk NR1 3LA
tel. (0603) 24817/25369

Phillips at 3 Opie Street, Norwich,
Norfolk NR1 3DP
tel. (0603) 616426

Nottingham:
Neales of Nottingham, 192 Mansfield Road,
Nottingham,
Nottinghamshire NG1 3HX
tel. (0602) 624141

Walker Walton Hanson, Byard Lane,
Bridlesmith Gate,
Nottingham, Nottinghamshire NG1 2GL
tel. (0602) 54272

Oxford:
Mallams, 24 St Michael's Street, Oxford,
Oxfordshire OX1 2DS
tel. (0865) 241358

Phillips, Incorporating Brooks, Fine Art Auctioneers, 39 Park End Street, Oxford,
Oxfordshire OX1 1JD
tel. (0865) 723524/5

Par:
Phillips Cornwall, Cornubia Hall, Par,
Cornwall PL24 2AQ
tel. (072 681) 2271

Penzance:
W.H. Lane & Sons, Central Auction Rooms,
Penzance, Cornwall TR18 2QT
tel. (0736) 61447/8

Perth:
Thomas Love & Sons Ltd, 52-54 Canal Street,
St John's Place, Perth, Perthshire PH1 5SU
tel. (0738) 24111

Pulborough:
Sotheby's in Sussex, Station Road,
Pulborough, West Sussex RH20 1AJ
tel. (07982) 3831

Reading:
Holloways, 12 High Street, Streatley, Reading,
Berkshire RG8 9HY
tel. (0491) 872318

Retford:
Henry Spencer & Sons, 20 The Square,
Retford, Nottinghamshire DN22 6DJ
tel. (0777) 708633

Rhyl:
C. Wesley Haslam & Son, St Helens Place,
High Street, Rhyl, Clwyd LL18 1TR
tel. (0745) 4467/8

Ryde:
Steadman & Way, Town Hall
Chambers, Lind Street, Ryde, Isle of Wight
PO33 2NQ
tel. (0983) 62255

St Ives:
Prudential Property Services (Fine Arts and
Chattels), The Saleroom, The Market, St Ives,
Huntingdon, Cambridgeshire
tel. (0480) 68144

Salisbury:
Woolley & Wallis, The Castle Auction Mart,
Castle Street, Salisbury, Wiltshire SP1 3SU
tel. (0722) 21711

Sandbach:
Andrew, Hilditch & Son, 19 The Square,
Sandbach, Cheshire CW11 0AT
tel. (093 67) 2048/7246

Scarborough:
.C. Chapman & Son, The Auction Mart,
North Street, Scarborough,
North Yorkshire YO11 1DL
tel. (0723) 72424

Selby:
Stephenson & Son, 43 Gowthorpe, Selby, North Yorkshire YO8 0HE
tel. (0757) 706707

Sevenoaks:
Parsons, Welch & Cowell, 129 High Street, Sevenoaks, Kent TN132 1UU
tel. (0732) 451211/4

Shepton Mallet:
Cooper & Tanner Ltd.,
44A Commercial Road, Shepton Mallet, Somerset BA4 5DN
tel. (0749) 2607

Shrewsbury:
Hall, Wateridge & Owen, Agricultural Auction House, Welsh Bridge,
Shrewsbury, Salop SY1 14L
tel. (0743) 25122

Sidmouth:
Peter J. Eley, Western House, 98-100 High Street, Sidmouth, Devon EX10 8EF
tel. (039 55) 2552

Sleaford:
William H. Brown, Northgate House, Sleaford, Lincolnshire NG34 7BZ
tel. (0529) 306868

Prudential Property Services,
67 Northgate, Sleaford,
Lincolnshire NG34 7AB
tel. (0529) 302946

Southsea:
D.M. Nesbit & Co., 7 Clarendon Road, Southsea, Hampshire PO5 2ED
tel. (0705) 820785/6

Stamford:
Henry Spencer & Sons, 38 St Mary's Street, Stamford, Lincolnshire PE9 2DS
tel. (0780) 52136

Sutton-in-Ashfield:
C.B. Sheppard & Son, The Auction Gallery, Chatsworth Street,
Sutton-in-Ashfield, Nottinghamshire
tel. (0773) 872419

Taunton:
W.R.J. Greenslade & Co., Priory Saleroom, Winchester Street,
Taunton, Somerset TA1 1RN
tel. (0823) 77121

Tenterden:
John Hogbin & Son, 53 High Street, Tenterden, Kent TN30 6BG
tel. (058 06) 3200

Thrapston:
Southam & Sons, Corn Exchange, Thrapston, nr Kettering,
Northamptonshire NN14 4JJ
tel. (080 12) 2409

Torquay:
Bearnes, Rainbow, Avenue Road, Torquay, Devon TQ2 5TG
tel. (0803) 26277

Wakefield:
Laidlaws, Crown Court, Wood Street, Wakefield, West Yorkshire WF1 2SU
tel. (0924) 75301

Wickham Market:
Abbotts (East Anglia) Ltd, The Hill, Wickham Market, nr Woodbridge,
Suffolk IP13 0QX
tel. (0728) 746321

Winchester:
Pearsons, Walcote Chambers, High Street, Winchester,
Hampshire SO23 9AB
tel. (0962) 62515

Wirral:
Kingsley & Co., 3-4 The Quadrant, Hoylake, Wirral,
Merseyside L47 2EE
tel. (051 632) 5821

Wokingham:
Martin & Pole, 5a & 7 Broad Street, Wokingham, Berkshire RG11 1AY
tel. (0734) 780777

Worcester:
Griffiths & Co, 57 Foregate Street, Worcester, Hereford and Worcester WR1 1DZ
tel. (0905) 26464

Andrew Grant, St Martin's House, St Mark's Close, Cherry Orchard,
Worcester, Hereford and Worcester WR5 3DT
tel. (0905) 357547

Worthing:
R.H. Ellis & Sons, 44-46 High Street, Worthing, Sussex BN11 1LL
tel. (0903) 38999

Wrexham:
Wingett & Son, 24-25 Chester Street, Wrexham, Clwyd LL18 8BP
tel. (0978) 353553/55245

Appendix II
A List of National and Regional Art Galleries and Art Collections in Great Britain

Greater London:
Air Gallery, 125-9 Shaftesbury Avenue, London WC2H 8AD
tel. (01) 240 3149

Bankside Gallery, 48 Hopton Street, Blackfriars, London SE1 9JH
tel. (01) 928 7521

Barbican Art Gallery, Barbican Centre, London EC2Y 8DS
tel. (01) 638 4141, ext. 306

British Museum, Department of Prints and Drawings, Great Russell Street, London, WC1B 3DG
tel. (01) 636 1555

Camden Arts Centre, Arkwright Road, London, NW3 6DG
tel. (01) 435 2643/5224

Canada House Gallery, Canada House, Trafalgar Square, London SW1Y 5BJ
tel. (01) 629 9492, ext. 246

Chiswick House, Burlington Lane, Chiswick, London W4 2RP
tel. (01) 995 0508

Courtauld Institute Galleries, The University of London, Woburn Square, London WC1H 0AA. (The Courtauld will be moving to Somerset House, Strand, London WC2, in 1989.)
tel. (01) 580 1015/636 2095

Dulwich College Picture Gallery, College Road, Dulwich, London SE21 7BG
tel. (01) 693 8000

Fenton House, Windmill Hill, London NW3 6RT
tel. (01) 435 3471

Forty Hall Museum, Forty Hill, Enfield, Middlesex EN2 9HA
tel. (01) 363 8196

Foundling Hospital Art Treasures (The Thomas Coram Foundation), 40 Brunswick Square, London WC1N 1AZ
tel. (01) 278 2424

Geffrye Museum, Kingsland Road, London E2 8AE
tel. (01) 739 8368

Hampton Court Palace, East Molesey, Surrey KT8 9AU
tel. (01) 977 8441

Hayward Gallery, South Bank Centre, Belvedere Road, South Bank, London SE1 8XZ
tel. (01) 928 3144/261 0127 (*recorded information*)

Hogarth's House, Hogarth Road, Great West Road, London W4 2QN
tel. (01) 994 6757

Imperial War Museum, Lambeth Road, London SE1 6HZ
tel. (01) 735 8922

Kenwood (The Iveagh Bequest), Hampstead Lane, Hampstead, London NW3 7UR
tel. (01) 348 1286

Leighton House Art Gallery and Museum, 12 Holland Park Road, Kensington, London W14 8LZ
tel. (01) 602 3316

Linley Sambourne House, 18 Stafford Terrace, Kensington, London W8
tel. (01) 994 1019

Marble Hill House, Richmond Road, Twickenham, London TW1 3DJ
tel. (01) 892 5115

Mall Galleries, Federation of British Artists, The Mall, London SW1Y 5BD
tel. (01) 930 6488

National Gallery, Trafalgar Square, London WC2N 5DN
tel. (01) 839 3321/839 3526 (recorded information)

National Maritime Museum, Romney Road, Greenwich, London SE10 9NF
tel. (01) 858 4422

National Portrait Gallery, St Martin's Place, Charing Cross Road, London WC2H 0EH
tel. (01) 930 4832

Orleans House Gallery, Riverside, Twickenham, London TW1 3DJ
tel. (01) 892 0221

Osterley Park House, Isleworth, Middlesex TW7 4RB
tel. (01) 519 4296

The Queen's Gallery, Buckingham Palace Road, London SW1A 1AA
tel. (01) 930 4832

Ranger's House, Chesterfield Walk, Blackheath, London SE10
tel. (01) 853 0035

Royal Academy of Arts, Burlington House, Piccadilly, London W1V 0DS
tel. (01) 734 9052

Royal College of Art Galleries, Kensington Gore, London SW7 2EU
tel. (01) 584 5020

Royal College of Music, Department of Portraits, Prince Consort Road, South Kensington, London SW7 2BS
tel. (01) 589 3643

Royal Society of Painters in Watercolours; and Royal Society of Painter-Etchers and Engravers – see Bankside Gallery

Serpentine Gallery, Kensington Gardens, London W2 3XA
tel. (01) 402 6075/732 9072 (recorded information)

Sir John Soane's Museum, 13 Lincoln's Inn Fields, London WC2A 3BP
tel. (01) 405 2107

South London Art Gallery, Peckham Road, London SE5 8UH
tel. (01) 703 6120

Syon House, Brentford, Middlesex TW8 8JG
tel. (01) 560 0884

Tate Gallery, Millbank, London SW1P 4RG
tel. (01) 821 1313/821 7128 (recorded information)

Theatre Museum, Theatrical Paintings Gallery 1E Tavistock Street, Covent Garden, London WC2E 7PA
tel. (01) 836 7891

Tudor Barn Art Gallery, Well Hall Plesaunce, Well Hall Road, Eltham, London SE9 6SS
tel. (01) 850 2340

Victoria and Albert Museum, Cromwell Road, South Kensington, London SW7 2RL
tel. (01) 589 6351/581 4894 (recorded information)

Wallace Collection, Hertford House, Manchester Square, London W1M 6BM
tel. (01) 935 0687

Wellington Museum, Apsley House, Hyde Park Corner, London W1V 9FA
tel. (01) 499 5676

Whitechapel Art Gallery, 80-82 Whitechapel Road, London E1 7QX
tel. (01) 377 0107

William Morris Gallery, Water House, Lloyd Park, Forest Road, Walthamstow, London E17 4PP
tel. (01) 527 5544, ext. 4390

Woodlands Art Gallery, 90 Mycenae Road, Blackheath, London SE3 7SE
tel. (01) 858 4631

Aberdeen:
Aberdeen Art Gallery, Schoolhill, Aberdeen
AB9 1FQ
tel. (0224) 646333

Aberystwyth:
Arts Centre Gallery, Penglais, Aberystwyth,
Dyfed SY23 2DE
tel. (0970) 4277

The Catherine Lewis Gallery and Print Room,
The Hugh Owen Library, The University
College of Wales, Aberystwyth, Dyfed
tel. (0970) 3339/3591

Accrington:
Haworth Arts Gallery, Haworth Park,
Manchester Road, Accrington, Lancashire BB5
2JS
tel. (0254) 33782

Alloway:
MacLaurin Art Gallery, Rozelle Park,
Momument Road, Alloway, Ayrshire KA7
4NQ
tel. (0292) 43708

Alnwick:
Alnwick Castle, Alnwick, Northumberland
NE66 1NQ
tel. (0665) 2207

Alton:
Allen Gallery, 10 & 12 Church Street, Alton,
Hampshire GU23 2BW
tel. (0420) 82802

Andover:
The Andover Museum and Art Gallery, Church
Close, Andover, Hampshire SP10 1DP
tel. (0264) 66283

Arbroath:
Arbroath Art Gallery, Public Library, Hill
Terrace, Arbroath, Tayside DD11 1EJ
tel. (0241) 2248

Arundel:
Arundel Castle, Arundel, Sussex BN18 9AB
tel. (0903) 882173

Ashford:
Godinton House, Godinton Park, Ashford,
Kent TN23 3BW
tel. (0233) 20773

Aylesbury:
Buckinghamshire County Museum, Church
Street, Aylesbury, Buckinghamshire HP20 2QP
tel. (0296) 82158/88849

Waddesdon Manor, Aylesbury,
Buckinghamshire HP18 0JH
tel. (0296) 65211

Ayr:
MacLaurin Gallery and Rozelle House, Rozelle,
Strathclyde
tel. (0292) 45447

Ayr Art Gallery and Museum, Carnegie
Library, 12 Main Street, Ayr, Ayrshire KA8
8ED
tel. (0292) 81510

Badminton:
Badminton House, Badminton, Avon GL9 1DB
tel. (045 421) 202

Bakewell:
Chatsworth House, Bakewell, Derbyshire DE4
1PN
tel. (0246 88) 3430

Bangor:
University College of North Wales Art Gallery,
Fford Gwynedd, Bangor, Gwynedd LL57 1DT
tel. (0248) 51151, ext. 437

Barnard Castle:
The Bowes Museum, Barnard Castle, Co.
Durham DL12 8NP
tel. (083 33) 2139

Barnsley:
Cannon Hall Museum and Art Gallery,
Cawthorne, Barnsley, South Yorkshire S75
4AT
tel. (0226) 790270

Cooper Art Gallery, Church Street, Barnsley,
South Yorkshire S70 2AH
tel. (0226) 42905

Basingstoke:
Willis Museum and Art Gallery, Old Town
Hall, Market Place, Basingstoke, Hampshire
RG21 1DP
tel. (0256) 66283

Bath:
Holburne of Menstrie Museum, Great Pulteney
Street, Bath, Avon BA2 4DB
tel. (0225) 66669

Victoria Art Gallery, Bridge Street, Bath, Avon
BA1 2HD
tel. (0225) 28144

Batley:
Batley Art Gallery, Market Place, Batley, West Yorkshire WF17 5DA
tel. (0924) 473141

Beccles:
Beccles and District Museum, Newgate, Beccles, Suffolk NR34 9RH
tel. (0502) 712628

Bedford:
Cecil Higgins Art Gallery, Castle Close, Bedford MK40 3NY
tel. (0234) 211222

Beverley:
Beverley Museum and Art Gallery, Champney Road, Beverley, North Humberside HU17 9HL
tel. (0482) 882255

Bideford:
Burton Art Gallery, Victoria Park, Kingsley Road, Bideford, North Devon EX39 2QQ
tel. (023 72) 6711

Billingham:
Billingham Art Gallery, Billingham Town Centre, Billingham, Cleveland
tel. (0642) 555443

Birkenhead:
Williamson Art Gallery and Museum, Slatey Road, Birkenhead, Wirral, Merseyside L42 4UE
tel. (051 652) 4177

Birmingham:
Barber Institute of Fine Arts, University of Birmingham, Birmingham, West Midlands B15 2TS
tel. (021 472) 0962

City Museum and Art Gallery, Chamberlain Square, Birmingham, West Midlands B3 3DH
tel. (021 235) 2834

Blackburn:
Blackburn Museum and Art Gallery, Library Street, Blackburn, Lancashire BB1 7AJ
tel. (0254) 667130

Blackpool:
Grundy Art Gallery, Queen Street, Blackpool, Lancashire FY1 1PX
tel. (0253) 23977

Blair Atholl:
Blair Castle and Atholl Museum, Blair Atholl, Tayside
tel. (079 681) 207/356

Blickling:
Blickling Hall, Blickling, nr Norwich NR11 6NF
tel. (026 373) 3471

Bolton:
Bolton Museum and Art Gallery, Le Mans Crescent, Bolton, Lancashire BL1 1SA
tel. (0204) 22311, ext. 2191

Bootle:
Bootle Museum and Art Gallery, Oriel Road, Bootle, Merseyside L20 7AG
tel. (065 78) 922 4040, ext. 245

Boston:
Guildhall Museum, South Street, Boston, Lincolnshire PE21 6HT
tel. (0205) 65954

Russell-Cotes Art Gallery and Museum, East Cliff, Bournemouth, Dorset BH1 3AA
tel. (0202) 21009

Bradford:
Cartwright Hall Art Gallery, Lister Park, Bradford, West Yorkshire BD9 4NS
tel. (0274) 493313

Bramber:
St Mary's, Bramber, West Sussex BN4 3WE (A fifteenth-century timber-framed house with rare seventeenth-century panelling.)
tel. (0903) 816205

Brechin:
Brechin Museum, Public Library, St Ninian's Square, Brechin, Tayside DD9 7AA
tel. (035 62) 2687 (for inquiries)

Bridlington:
Bridlington Art Gallery and Museum, Sewerby Hall, Bridlington, North Humberside YO15 1EA
tel. (0262) 678225

Bridport:
Museum and Art Gallery, South Street, Bridport, Dorset DT6 3NZ
tel. (0308) 22116

Brigg:
Wrawby Moor Art Gallery, Elsham Hall Country Park, Brigg, South Humberside
tel. (0652) 8738

Brighton:
Art Gallery and Museum, Church Street, Brighton, East Sussex BN1 1VE
tel. (0273) 603005

The Royal Pavilion, Brighton, East Sussex BN1
1UE
tel. (0273) 603005

Bristol:
City of Bristol Museum and Art Gallery,
Queens Road, Clifton, Bristol, Avon BS8 1RL
tel. (0272) 299771

Brodick:
Brodick Castle, Brodick, Isle of Arran KA27
8HY
tel. (0770) 2202

Buckie:
Buckie Maritime Museum, Cluny Place,
Buckie, Grampian
tel. (0309) 73701

Burnley:
Towneley Hall Art Gallery and Museums,
Burnley, Lancashire BB11 3RQ
tel. (0282) 24213

Bury:
Bury Art Gallery and Museums, Manchester
Road, Bury, Lancashire BL9 0DG
tel. (061 764) 4110/4021

Buxton:
Buxton Museum and Art Gallery, Terrace
Road, Buxton, Derbyshire SK17 6DU
tel. (0928) 4658

Caernarfon:
Arfon Gallery, 16 Palace Street, Caernarfon,
Gwynedd LL55 1RR
tel. (0286) 2602

Cambridge:
Anglesey Abbey, Lode, Cambridge CB5 9EJ
tel. (0223) 352124

Kettle's Yard, Northampton Street, Cambridge
CB3 0AQ
tel. (0223) 352124

Fitzwilliam Museum, Trumpington Street,
Cambridge CB1 1RB
tel. (0223) 69501

Canterbury:
Royal Museum and Art Gallery, High Street,
Canterbury, Kent CT1 2JF
tel. (0227) 52747

Cardiff:
Burges Drawings Collection, Cardiff Castle,
Cardiff, South Glamorgan CF1 2RB (*Written
application only to:* Director of Administration
and Legal Services.)
tel. (0222) 822084

National Museum of Wales, Cathays Park,
Cardiff, South Glamorgan CF1 3NP
tel. (0222) 397951

Carlisle:
Carlisle Museum and Art Gallery, Tullie
House, Castle Street, Carlisle, Cumbria CA3
8TP
tel. (0228) 34781

Caterham:
East Surrey Museum, 1 Stafford Road,
Caterham, Surrey CR3 6JG
tel. (0883) 40275

Cavendish:
Nether Hall Museum and Art Gallery,,
Cavendish, Suffolk
tel. (0787) 280221

Channel Islands:
Candie Gardens, St Peter Port, Guernsey,
Channel Islands
tel. (0481) 26518

Castle Cornet, St Peter Port, Guernsey,
Channel Islands
tel. (0482) 21657

Coach House Gallery, Les Islets, St Peters,
Guernsey, Channel Islands
tel. (0481) 65339

Jersey Museum, 9 Pier Road, St Helier, Jersey,
Channel Islands
tel. (0534) 75940

Sir Francis Cook Gallery, Route de la Trinité,
Augrès, Jersey, Channel Islands
tel. (0534) 63333

Chard:
Forde Abbey, Chard, Somerset TA20 4LU
tel. (0460) 2231

Cheltenham:
Cheltenham Art Gallery and Museum,
1 Clarence Street, Cheltenham,
Gloucestershire GL50 3JT
tel. (0242) 37431/2

Sudeley Castle, Winchcombe, Cheltenham,
Gloucestershire GL54 5JD
tel. (0242) 602308

Chepstow:
St Arvans Gallery, St Arvans, nr Chepstow,
Gwent
tel. (029 12) 5997

Chester:
Grosvenor Museum, Grosvenor Street, Chester
CH1 2DD
tel. (0244) 321616

Chichester:
Goodwood House, Goodwood, Chichester,
West Sussex PO18 0PX
tel. (0243) 527107

Pallant House Gallery, 9 North Pallant,
Chichester, West Sussex
tel. (0243) 774557

Chorley:
Astley Hall Art Gallery and Museum, Astley
Park, Chorley, Lancashire PR7 1NP
tel. (025 72) 62166

Colchester:
The Minories, 74 High Street, Colchester,
Essex CO1 1UE
tel. (0206) 77067

Colne:
British in India Museum, Sun Street, Colne,
Lancashire BB8 0JJ
tel. (0282) 63129

Coniston:
Brantwood (home of John Ruskin), Coniston,
Cumbria LA21 8AD
tel. (0966) 4396

The Ruskin Museum, The Institute, Coniston,
Cumbria LA21 8DU
tel. (053 94) 41387

Conwy:
Plas Mawr, High Street, Conwy, Gwynedd
LL32 8DE
tel. (049 263) 3413

Cookham-on-Thames:
Stanley Spencer Gallery, King's Hall,
Cookham-on-Thames, Berkshire SL6 9SJ
tel. (062 85) 26557

Coventry:
Herbert Art Gallery and Museum, Jordan Well,
Coventry, West Midlands CV1 5RW
tel. (0203) 25555, ext. 2315

Culross:
Dunimarle Museum, Culross, Fife
tel. (0383) 229

Darlington:
Darlington Art Gallery, Crown Street,
Darlington, Co. Durham DL1 1ND
tel. (0325) 62034

Dedham:
The Sir Alfred Munnings Art Museum, Castle
House, Dedham, Colchester, Essex CO7 6AZ
tel. (0206) 322127

Derby:
Derby Museum and Art Gallery, The Strand,
Derby DE1 1BS
tel. (0332) 31111, ext. 781

Sudbury Hall and Museum, Sudbury,
Derbyshire DE6 5HT
tel. (028 378) 305

Devizes:
Devizes Museum, 41 Long Street, Devizes,
Wiltshire SN10 1NS
tel. (0380) 71279

Ditchling:
Ditchling Museum, Church Lane, Ditchling,
West Sussex
tel. (079 18) 4744

Doncaster:
Doncaster Museum and Art Gallery, Chequer
Road, Doncaster, South Yorkshire DN1 2AE
tel. (0302) 734287

Douglas:
Manx Museum and Art Gallery, Douglas, Isle
of Man
tel. (0624) 5522

Dudley:
Dudley Museum and Art Gallery, St James's
Road, Dudley, West Midlands DY1 1HU
tel. (0384) 55433

Dumfries:
Museum of the Royal Burgh of Sanquhar, The
Tolbooth, Dumfries DG4 6BL
tel. (0659) 2303

Dundee:
McManus Galleries, Albert Square, Dundee,
Angus DD1 1DA
tel. (0382) 25492/3

James Guthrie Orchar Art Gallery, Beach
House, 31 Beach Crescent, Broughty Ferry,
Dundee, Angus DD1 1B8
tel. (0382) 77337

Dunfermline:
Pittencrief House Museum, Pittencrief Park,
Dunfermline, Fife (*correspondence* c/o
Dunfermline Museum, Viewfield,
Dunfermline, Fife KY12 7HY)
tel. (0383) 722935/721814

Eastbourne:
Towner Art Gallery, Manor Gardens, Old Town, Eastbourne, East Sussex BN20 8BB
tel. (0323) 21635

Edge Hill:
Upton House, Edge Hill, Warwickshire
tel. (029 587) 266

Edinburgh:
City Art Centre, 2 Market Street, Edinburgh, Lothian
tel. (031) 225 2424, ext. 6650

The Fruitmarket Gallery, 29 Market Street, Edinburgh, Lothian EH1 1DF
tel. (031) 225 2383

National Gallery of Scotland, The Mound, Edinburgh, Lothian EH1 1SR
tel. (031) 556 8921

Scottish National Gallery of Modern Art, Belford Road, Edinburgh, Lothian EH3 5LR
tel. (031) 332 3754

Scottish National Portrait Gallery, 1 Queen Street, Edinburgh, Lothian EH2 1JD
tel. (031) 556 8921

Exeter:
Royal Albert Memorial Museum and Art Gallery, Queen Street, Exeter, Devon EX4 3RX
tel. (0392) 265858

Falmouth:
Falmouth Art Gallery, The Moor, Falmouth, Cornwall
tel. (0326) 313863

Faringdon:
Buscot Park, nr Faringdon, Oxfordshire tel. (0367) 20786

Filkins:
The Cross Tree Gallery, Filkins, Gloucestershire
tel. (036) 786 494

Folkestone:
Arts Centre, The Metropole, The Leas, Folkestone, Kent
tel. (0303) 55070

Folkestone Museum and Art Gallery, Grace Hill, Folkestone, Kent GT20 1HD
tel. (0303) 57583

Ford:
Lady Waterford Hall, Ford Village, Northumberland
tel. (089 082) 30224

Fordingbridge:
Braemore House, Braemore, nr Fordingbridge, Hampshire SP6 2DE
tel. (072 52) 270233

Forfar:
Forfar Museum and Art Gallery, Meffan Institute, Forfar, Angus DD8 1BB
tel. (0307) 3468

Gateshead:
Shipley Art Gallery, Prince Consort Road South, Gateshead, Tyne and Wear NE8 4JB
tel. (091) 477 1495

Glasgow:
The Burrell Collection, Pollok Country Park, Glasgow, Strathclyde G43 1AT
tel. (041) 649 7151

Collins Gallery, University of Strathclyde, Richmond Street, Glasgow, Strathclyde G1 1XQ
tel. (041) 552 4400, ext. 2682/2416

Glasgow Art Gallery and Museum, Kelvingrove, Glasgow, Strathclyde G3 8AG
tel. (041) 357 3929

Hunterian Art Gallery, Hillhead Street, Glasgow University, Glasgow, Strathclyde G12 8QQ
tel. (041) 330 5431

Pollok House, Pollok Country Park, Glasgow, Strathclyde G43 1AT
tel. (041) 552 8819

Gloucester:
City Museum and Art Gallery, Brunswick Road, Gloucester, Gloucestershire GL1 1HP
tel. (0452) 24131

Grantham:
Belton House, Belton, Grantham, Lincolnshire NG32 2LP
tel. (0476) 66116

Goole:
Goole Museum and Art Gallery, Goole Library, Market Square, Goole, Humberside DN14 5AA
tel. (0405) 2187

Grasmere:
Dove Cottage and Wordsworth Museum, Grasmere, Cumbria LA22 9SG
tel. (096 65) 544/547

The Heaton Cooper Studio, Grasmere, Cumbria LA22 9SX
tel. (096 65) 280

Great Yarmouth:
Exhibition Galleries, Central Library, Tolhouse Street, Great Yarmouth, Norfolk NR30 2SQ
tel. (0493) 858900

Maritime Museum for East Anglia, 25 Marine Parade, Great Yarmouth, Norfolk NR30 2EN
tel. (0493) 2267

Greenock:
The McLean Museum and Art Gallery, 9 Union Street, West End, Greenock, Strathclyde PA16 9JH
tel. (0475) 23741

Grimsby:
Doughty Museum, Town Hall Square, Grimsby, Humberside DN31 1HU
tel. (0472) 59161

Welholme Galleries, Welholme Road, Grimsby, Humberside DN32 9LP
tel. (0472) 242000

Guildford:
Guildford House Art Gallery, 155 High Street, Guildford, Surrey GU1 3AJ
tel. (0483) 503406, ext. 3531

The Watts Gallery, Compton, nr Guildford, Surrey GU1 1DQ
tel. (0483) 810235

Hailsham:
Michelham Priory, Upper Dicker, Hailsham, Sussex BN27 3QS
tel. (0323) 844224

Halifax:
Bankfield Museum and Art Gallery, Akroyd Park, Halifax, West Yorkshire
tel. (0422) 54823/52334

Smith Art Gallery, Halifax Road, Brighouse, Halifax, West Yorkshire
tel. (0484) 719222

Harrogate:
Harrogate Art Gallery, Library Buildings, Victoria Avenue, Harrogate, North Yorkshire (*correspondence* c/o Museum Service, Council Offices, Harrogate, North Yorkshire HG1 2SG)
tel. (0423) 503340

Ripley Castle, Ripley, nr Harrogate, North Yorkshire HG3 3AY
tel. (0423) 770186

Hartlepool:
Gray Art Gallery and Museum, Clarence Road, Hartlepool, Cleveland TS24 8BT
tel. (0429) 268916

Hastings:
Hastings Museum and Art Gallery, St John's Place, Cambridge Road, Hastings, East Sussex TN34 1ET
tel. (0424) 721202

Hatfield:
Hatfield House, Hatfield, Hertfordshire AL9 5NQ
tel. (070 72) 62823

Havant:
The Havant Museum, East Street, Havant, Hampshire
tel. (0705) 451155

Haverfordwest:
The Castle Museum and Art Gallery, Haverfordwest, Dyfed SA61 2EF
tel. (0437) 3708

Graham Sutherland Gallery, The Rhos, Haverfordwest, Dyfed SA62 4AS
tel. (0437) 86296

Hawick:
Museum and Art Gallery, Wilton Park Lodge, Hawick, Borders TD9 7LJ
tel. (0450) 73457

Henley-on-Thames:
Historic House and Museum, Marian Fathers, Fawley Court, Henley-on-Thames, Oxfordshire
tel. (0491) 574717

Hereford:
Churchill Gardens Museum, Venn's Lane, Hereford HR1 1DE
tel. (0432) 267409

Hereford Museum and Art Gallery, Broad Street, Hereford HR4 9AU
tel. (0432) 268121, ext. 207

Hitchin:
Hitchin Museum and Art Gallery, Paynes Park, Hitchin, Hertfordshire SG5 1EQ
tel. (0462) 34476

Hove:
Hove Museum of Art, 19 New Church Road, Hove, East Sussex BN3 4AB
tel. (0273) 779410

Huddersfield:
Huddersfield Art Gallery, Princess Alexandra Walk, Huddersfield, West Yorkshire HD1 2SU
tel. (0484) 513808

Hull:
Ferens Art Gallery, Queen Victoria Square, Hull, Humberside HU1 3RA
tel. (0482) 222750

Posterngate Art Gallery, 6 Posterngate, Hull, Humberside HU1 2JN
tel. (0482) 222745

Ilfracombe:
Ilfracombe Museum, Wilder Road, Devon EX34 8AF
tel. (0271) 36541

Ilkley:
Manor House Museum and Art Gallery, Castle Yard, Ilkley, West Yorkshire LS29 2DT
tel. (0943) 3600066

Inveraray:
Inveraray Castle, Cherry Park, Inverary, Strathclyde
tel. (0499) 5235

Inverness:
Inverness Museum and Art Gallery, Castle Wynd, Inverness, Highland IV2 3ED
tel. (0463) 237114

Isle of Wight:
The Ruskin Gallery, Bembridge School, Isle of Wight
tel. (0983) 872101 (*view by appointment only*)

Ryde Gallery, Ryde Library, George Street, Ryde, Isle of Wight
tel. (0983) 672170

Ipswich:
Christchurch Mansion and Wolsey Art Gallery, Christchurch Park, Ipswich, Suffolk
tel. (0473) 53246

Keighley:
Cliffe Castle Museum and Art Gallery, Keighley, West Yorkshire BD20 6LH
tel. (0535) 664184

Kendal:
Abbot Hall Art Gallery, Abbot Hall, Kendal, Cumbria
tel. (0539) 22464

Keswick:
Fitz Park Museum and Art Gallery, Station Road, Keswick, Cumbria
tel. (0596) 73263

Kettering:
Alfred East Art Gallery, Sheep Street, Kettering, Northamptonshire
tel. (0536) 85211

Kidderminster:
Art Gallery, Hartlebury Castle, Market Street, Kidderminster, Hereford & Worcester DY11 7ZX
tel. (0562) 66610

Kilmarnock:
Dick Institute Museum and Art Gallery, Elmbank Avenue, Kilmarnock, Strathclyde KA1 3BU
tel. (0563) 26401

King's Lynn:
The Fermoy Centre, King Street, King's Lynn, Norfolk PE30 1HA
tel. (0553) 773578

Kirkaldy:
Kirkaldy Museum and Art Gallery, By Kirkaldy Railway Station, Kirkaldy, Fife
tel. (0592) 260732

Kirkintilloch:
The Auld Kirk Museum, Cowgate, Kirkintilloch, Strathclyde
tel. (041) 775 1185

Kirkcudbright:
Broughton House, High Street, Kirkcudbright, Dumfries and Galloway
tel. (0557) 30437

Knutsford:
Tatton Hall, Tatton Park, Knutsford, Cheshire WA1 6QL
tel. (0565) 3155

Lancaster:
Lancaster City Museum, Old Town Hall, Market Square, Lancaster LA1 1HT
tel. (0524) 64637

Leamington Spa:
Leamington Spa Art Gallery and Museum, Avenue Road, Leamington Spa, Warwickshire CV31 3PP
tel. (0926) 26559

Leeds:
City Art Gallery, The Headrow, Leeds, West Yorkshire LS1 3AA
tel. (0532) 647321

Harewood House, Harewood, nr Leeds, West Yorkshire LS17 9LQ
tel. (0532) 886225

Lotherton Hall, Aberford, Leeds, West Yorkshire LS25 3EB
tel. (097) 332 259

Leek:
Leek Art Gallery, Stockwell Street, Leek,
Staffordshire ST13 6DW
tel. (0538) 399181

Leicester:
Leicestershire Museum and Art Gallery, New
Walk, Leicester LE1 6TD
tel. (0533) 554100

Leigh:
Turnpike Gallery, Leigh, Greater Manchester
tel. (0942) 679407

Letchworth:
Letchworth Museum and Art Gallery,
Broadway, Letchworth, Hertfordshire SG6 3PD
tel. (0462) 683149

Lewes:
Firle Place, Lewes, Sussex BN8 6LP
tel. (607915) 9256

Lindisfarne:
Lindisfarne Castle, Holy Island,
Northumberland
tel. (0289) 89253

Lincoln:
Doddington Hall, Doddington, Lincoln LN6
0RU
tel. (0522) 74 227

Usher Art Gallery, Lindum Road, Lincoln LN2
1NN
tel. (0522) 27980

Littlehampton:
Littlehampton Museum, 12a River Road,
Littlehampton, West Sussex LN2 1NN
tel. (0903) 715149

Liverpool:
Bluecoat Gallery, Bluecoat Chambers, School
Lane, Liverpool, Merseyside L1 3BX
tel. (051) 709 8659

Sudley Art Gallery, Mossley Hill Road,
Liverpool, Merseyside L18 8BX
tel. (051) 207 0001

University of Liverpool Art Gallery,
3 Abercromby Square, Liverpool, Merseyside
L69 3BX
tel. (051) 709 6022, ext. 3170

Walker Art Gallery, Liverpool, Merseyside
L3 8EL
tel. (051) 207 0001

Llandudno:
Mostyn Art Gallery, 12 Vaughan Street,
Llandudno, Gwynedd
tel. (0492) 79201

Llanelli:
Parc Howard Art Gallery and Museum, Parc
Howard, Llanelli, Dyfed SA15 3JU
tel. (0554) 773538

Public Library Gallery, Llanelli, Dyfed
tel. (0554) 773538

Llanfairpwll:
Plas Newydd, Llanfairpwll, Anglesey LL61 6EQ
tel. (0248) 86 795

Luton:
Luton Museum and Art Gallery, Wardown
Park, Luton, Bedfordshire LU2 7HA
tel. (0582) 36941/2

Luton Hoo (The Wernher Collection), Luton,
Bedfordshire LU2 7HA
tel. (0582) 22955

Lyme Regis:
Philpot Museum, Bridge Street, Lyme Regis,
Dorset DT7 3QA
tel. (02974) 3127

Lytham St Anne's:
St Anne's Art Gallery, Public Offices, Clifton
Drive South, Lytham St Anne's, Lancashire
FY8 1LH
tel. (0253) 721222

Macclesfield:
West Park Museum and Art Gallery, Prestbury
Road, Macclesfield, Cheshire SK10 3BJ
tel. (0625) 24067

Maidenhead:
Henry Reitlinger Bequest, Oldfield, Riverside,
Guards Club Road, Maidenhead, Berkshire SL6
8DN
tel. (0628) 21818

Maidstone:
Maidstone Museum and Art Gallery, St Faith's
Street, Maidstone, Kent ME14 4HU
tel. (0622) 54497

Manchester:
Athenaeum Gallery, Princess Street,
Manchester M1 4HR
tel. (061) 236 9422

City Art Gallery, Mosley Street, Manchester
M2 3JL
tel. (061) 236 9422

Fletcher Moss Art Gallery and Museum, The
Old Parsonage, Stenner Lane, Didsbury,
Manchester M20 8AU
tel. (061) 236 9422

Heaton Hall, Heaton Park, Prestwich,
Manchester M25 5SW
tel. (061) 236 9422

Holden Gallery, Manchester Polytechnic,
Cavendish Street, All Saints, Manchester M15
6BR
tel. (061) 228 6171

Portico Library Gallery, 57 Mosley Street,
Manchester M2 3HY
tel. (061) 236 6785

Queen's Park Art Gallery and Museum,
Queen's Park, Harpurhey, Manchester M19
1SH
tel. (061) 205 2121

Whitworth Art Gallery, University of
Manchester, Oxford Road, Manchester M15
6ER
tel. (061) 273 4865

Wythenshawe Hall, Wythenshawe Park,
Northenden, Manchester M23 0AB
tel. (061) 236 9422

Mansfield:
Mansfield Museum and Art Gallery, Leeming
Street, Mansfield, Nottinghamshire
NG18 1NG
tel. (0623) 663088

Market Harborough:
Rockingham Castle, Rockingham, Market
Harborough, Leicestershire LE16 8TH
tel. (0536) 70 240

Merthyr Tydfil:
Cyfarthfa Castle Art Gallery and Museum,
Cyfarthfa Park, Merthyr Tydfil, Mid
Glamorgan CF47 8RE
tel. (0685) 3112

Middlesbrough:
Cleveland Gallery, Victoria Road,
Middlesbrough, Cleveland TS1 3QS
tel. (0642) 248155, ext. 3375

Middlesbrough Art Gallery, Linthorpe Road,
Middlesbrough, Cleveland TS1 3QY
tel. (0642) 247445

Milngavie:
Lillie Art Gallery, Station Road, Milngavie,
Strathclyde G62 8BZ
tel. (041) 956 2351

Montacute:
Montacute House, Montacute, Somerset TA15
6XP
tel. (0935) 823289

Montrose:
Montrose Museum, Panmure Place, Montrose,
Tayside (*correspondence* c/o The Signal Tower
Museum, Ladyloan, Arbroath, Tayside DN11
1PU)
tel. (0674) 73232

Morpeth:
Wallington Hall, Cambo, Morpeth,
Northumberland
tel. (0670) 74 283

Newark:
Newark Museum, Appleton Gate, Newark,
Nottinghamshire NG24 1JY
tel. (0636) 702358

Newcastle-under-Lyme:
Hobbergate Art Gallery, The Brampton,
Newcastle-under-Lyme, Staffordshire ST5 0QP
tel. (0782) 619705

Newcastle-upon-Tyne:
Greys Gallery, 77-79 High Street, Gosforth,
Newcastle-upon-Tyne, Tyne and Wear
tel. (091) 284 735

Hatton Gallery, Department of Fine Art, The
University of Newcastle-upon-Tyne, Kings
Road, Newcastle-upon-Tyne, Tyne and Wear
NE1 7RU
tel. (091) 2328511

Laing Art Gallery, Higham Place, Newcastle-
upon-Tyne, Tyne and Wear NE1 8AG
tel. (0632) 327734/326989

Newmarket:
The National Horseracing Museum, High
Street, Newmarket, Suffolk
tel. (0638) 667333

Newlyn:
Newlyn Art Gallery, Newlyn, Cornwall
tel. (0736) 63715

Newport:
Newport Museum and Art Gallery, John Frost
Square, Newport, Gwent NPT 1PA
tel. (0633) 840064

Northampton:
Althorp House, Althorp, nr Northampton NN7
4HG
tel. (061) 125 209

Castle Ashby House, nr Northampton NN7 1LJ
tel. (060) 129 233

Central Museum and Art Gallery, Guildhall
Road, Northampton NN1 1DP
tel. (0604) 34881

Norwich:
Norwich Castle Museum, Norwich NR1 3JU
tel. (0603) 611277, ext. 279

Sainsbury Centre for the Visual Arts,
University of East Anglia, Norwich NR4 7TJ
tel. (0603) 56060

Nottingham:
Nottingham Castle Museum, Nottingham
NG1 6EL
tel. (0602) 411881

University Art Gallery, Department of Fine
Art, Portland Building, University Park,
Nottingham NG7 2RD
tel. (0602) 506101, ext 2253

Nuneaton:
Arbury Hall, Windmill Hill, Astley, nr
Nuneaton, Warwickshire CV10 7PZ
tel. (0676) 40529

Nuneaton Museum and Art Gallery, Riversley
Park, Nuneaton, Warwickshire CV11 5TU
tel. (0203) 376473

Oldham:
Oldham Art Gallery, Union Street, Oldham,
Greater Manchester OL1 1DN
tel. (061) 678 4651

Saddleworth Museum and Art Gallery, High
Street, Uppermill, Oldham, Greater
Manchester OL3 6HS
tel. (045) 77 4093

Oxford:
The Ashmolean Museum of Art and
Archaeology, Beaumont Street, Oxford OX1
2PH
tel. (0865) 278000

Christ Church Picture Gallery, Canterbury
Gate, Christ Church, Oxford OX1 1DP
tel. (0865) 276172

Museum of Modern Art, 30 Pembroke Street,
Oxford OX1 1BP
tel. (0865) 722733

Paisley:
Paisley Museum and Art Galleries, High Street,
Paisley, Strathclyde PA1 2BA
tel. (041) 889 3151

Penarth:
Turner House, Penarth, South Glamorgan
tel. (0222) 708870

Penzance:
Penlee House Museum Art Gallery, Penlee
Park, Penzance, Cornwall
tel. (0736) 63625/63405

Perth:
Perth Museum and Art Gallery, George Street,
Perth, Tayside
tel. (0738) 32488

Peterborough:
City Museum and Art Gallery, Priestgate,
Peterborough, Cambridgeshire PE1 1LF
tel. (0733) 43329

Petworth:
Petworth House, Petworth, West Sussex GU28
0AE
tel. (0798) 42207

Plymouth:
City Museum and Art Gallery, Drake Circus,
Plymouth, Devon PL4 8AJ
tel. (0752) 264878

Portsmouth:
Portsmouth City Museum and Art Gallery,
Museum Road, Old Portsmouth, Hampshire
PO1 2LJ
tel. (0705) 827261

Port Sunlight:
Lady Lever Art Gallery, Port Sunlight Village,
Wirral, Merseyside L62 5EQ
tel. (051) 645 3623

Preston:
Harris Museum and Art Gallery, Market
Square, Preston, Lancashire PR1 2PP
tel. (0772) 58248

Pulborough:
Parham Park, Pulborough, West Sussex RH20
4HS
tel. (090) 66 2021

Ramsgate:
Ramsgate Museum, Ramsgate Library,
Guildford Lawn, Ramsgate, Kent
tel. (0843) 53532

Reading:
Museum and Art Gallery, Blagrave Street,
Reading, Berkshire RG1 1QL
tel. (0734) 55911, ext. 2242

Stratfield Saye House, Stratfield Saye, nr
Reading, Berkshire RG7 2BZ
tel. (025) 688 601/666

Rhyl:
Rhyl Library, Museum and Arts Centre,
Church Street, Rhyl, Clwyd
tel. (0745) 53814/53833

Rochdale:
Rochdale Art Gallery, Rochdale, Lancashire
tel. (0706) 342154, exts. 764/269

Rochdale College of Arts and Design, Leo
Solomon Gallery, St Mary's Gate, Rochdale,
Lancashire OL12 6RY
tel. (0706) 34546

Rossendale:
Rossendale Museum, Whitaker Park,
Rawtenstall, Rossendale, Lancashire BB4 6RE
tel. (0706) 217777

Rothbury:
Cragside House, Rothbury, Northumberland
tel. (0669) 20333

Rotherham:
Art Gallery, Brian O'Malley Library and Arts
Centre, Walker Place, Rotherham, South
Yorkshire S65 1JH
tel. (0709) 382121, ext. 3569/3519

Rotherham Museum, Clifton Park, Rotherham,
South Yorkshire S65 2AA
tel. (0709) 382121, ext. 3569/3519

Rottingdean:
The Grange Art Gallery and Museum, The
Green, Rottingdean, East Sussex
tel. (0273) 31004

Royston:
Museum, Lower King Street, Royston,
Hertfordshire
tel. (0763) 42587

Rugby:
Rugby Library and Exhibition Gallery, St
Matthew's Street, Rugby, Warwickshire CV21
3BZ
tel. (0788) 2687/71813

St Andrews:
Archive of Popular Art and Culture in the
Twentieth Century, Department of Fine Arts,
University of St Andrews, Fife KY19 9AJ
tel. (0334) 815011

Crawford Centre for the Arts, University of St
Andrews, 93 North Street, St Andrews,
Fife KY16 9AL
tel. (0334) 76161, ext. 591

St Helens:
St Helens Museum and Art Gallery, College
Street, St Helens, Merseyside WA10 1TW
tel. (074) 24061, ext. 2959

St Ives:
Old Mariners Church, Norway Square, St Ives,
Cornwall
tel. (0736) 795582

Penwith Galleries, Back Road West, St Ives,
Cornwall TR26 1NL
tel. (0736) 705579

St Ives Museum, Wheal Dream, St Ives,
Cornwall TR26 1PR
tel. (0736) 706005

Salford:
Salford Museum and Art Gallery, The
Crescent, Peel Park, Salford, Greater
Manchester M5 4WU
tel. (061) 736 2649

Salisbury:
Salisbury Library Exhibition Galleries, Market
Place, Salisbury, Wiltshire SP1 1BL
tel. (0722) 24145

Wilton House, Wilton, nr Salisbury, Wiltshire
SP20 0BJ
tel. (0722) 743115

Scarborough:
Art Gallery, The Crescent, Scarborough, North
Yorkshire YO11 2PW
tel. (0723) 374753

Wood End Museum, The Crescent,
Scarborough, North Yorkshire YO11 2PW
tel. (0723) 367326

Scunthorpe:
Scunthorpe Borough Museum and Art Gallery,
Oswald Road, Scunthorpe, Humberside DN15
7BD
tel. (0724) 843533

Normanby Hall, Normanby, Scunthorpe,
Humberside DN15 9HT
tel. (0724) 720215

Sheffield:
Graves Art Gallery, Surrey Street, Sheffield,
South Yorkshire
S1 1X7
tel. (0742) 734781

Mappin Art Gallery, Weston Park, Sheffield, South Yorkshire
S10 1XZ
tel. (0742) 26281/754091

Ruskin Gallery, 101 Norfolk Street, Sheffield, South Yorkshire S1 2JE
tel. (0742) 734781

Shrewsbury:
Shrewsbury Borough Art Gallery, Castle Gate, Shrewsbury
SY1 1LZ
tel. (0743) 54811

Southampton:
Southampton Art Gallery, Civic Centre, Southampton, Hampshire SO9 4XF
tel. (0703) 832769

Southport:
Atkinson Art Gallery, Lord Street, Southport, Merseyside PR8 1DH
tel. (0704) 33133, ext. 2111

Botanic Gardens Museum, Churchtown, Southport, Merseyside PR9 7NB
tel. (0704) 27547

South Queensferry:
Hopetoun House, South Queensferry, Lothian
EH30 9SL
tel. (031) 331 2451

South Shields:
Museum and Art Gallery, Ocean Road, South Shields, Tyne and Wear NE33 2AU
tel. (091) 4568740

Stafford:
Shugborough Mansion House, Milford, nr Stafford
tel. (0889) 881388

Stafford Museum and Art Gallery, The Green, Stafford ST17 4BH
tel. (0785) 57303

Stalybridge:
The Astley Cheetham Art Gallery, Trinity Street, Stalybridge, Greater Manchester
tel. (061) 338 2708

Stamford:
Burghley House, Stamford, Lincolnshire PE9 3JX
tel. (0780) 3131

Stirling:
MacRobert Centre Art Gallery, University of Stirling, Stirling, Central
tel. (0786) 3171, ext. 2549

Stirling Smith Art Gallery and Museum, 40 Albert Place, Stirling, Central FK8 2RQ
tel. (0786) 71917

Stockport:
Bramhall Hall, Bramhall Park, Bramhall, Stockport, Cheshire SK7 3NX
tel. (061) 485 3708

Stockport War Memorial Art Gallery, Wellington Road South, Stockport, Greater Manchester
tel. (061) 480 9433

Stockton-on-Tees:
Preston Hall Museum, Yarm Road, Stockton-on-Tees, Cleveland
tel. (0642) 781184

Stoke-on-Trent:
City Museum and Art Gallery, Bethesda Street, Hanley, Stoke-on-Trent, Staffordshire ST1 3DE
tel. (0782) 202173

Stromness:
The Pier Arts Centre, Stromness, Orkney
tel. (0856) 850209

Sudbury:
Gainsborough's House, 46 Gainsborough Street, Sudbury, Suffolk CO10 6EV
tel. (0787) 72958

Sunderland:
Sunderland Museum and Art Gallery, Borough Road, Sunderland, Tyne and Wear SR1 1PP
tel. (0783) 51 41235

Swansea:
Glynn Vivian Art Gallery and Museum, Alexandra Road, Swansea, West Glamorgan
SA1 5DZ
tel. (0792) 55006

Swindon:
Museum and Art Gallery, Bath Road, Swindon, Wiltshire SN1 4BA
tel. (0793) 26161, ext. 3129

Tenby:
Tenby Museum and Picture Gallery, Castle Hill, Tenby, Dyfed
tel. (0834) 2809

Thetford:
Euston Hall, Euston, nr Thetford, Norfolk IP24 2QW
tel. (0842) 3281

Thirsk:
Sion Hill Hall, Kirby Wiske, Thirsk, North Yorkshire
tel. (0845) 587206

Torquay:
Torre Abbey Mansion House, The King's Drive, Torquay, Devon TQ2 5JX
tel. (0803) 23593

Truro:
County Museum and Art Gallery, River Street, Truro, Cornwall TR1 2SJ
tel. (0872) 72205

Tunbridge Wells:
Tunbridge Wells Museum and Art Gallery, Civic Centre, Mount Pleasant, Tunbridge Wells, Kent TN1 1RS
tel. (0892) 26121, ext. 171

Wakefield:
Heath Hall, Wakefield, West Yorkshire WF1 5SL
tel. (0924) 76710

Wakefield Art Gallery, Wentworth Terrace, Wakefield, West Yorkshire
tel. (0924) 370211, ext. 8013

Wallasey:
Wallasey Museum and Exhibition Hall, Wallasey Library, Earlston Road, Wallasey, Merseyside L45 5DX
tel. (051) 639 2334/5

Walsall:
Museum and Art Gallery, Lichfield Street, Walsall, West Midlands WS1 1TR
tel. (0922) 21244, ext. 3124/3115

Waltham Abbey:
Epping Forest District Museum, 39-41 Sun Street, Waltham Abbey, Essex EN9 1EL
tel. (0992) 716882

Warminster:
Longleat House, Warminster, Wiltshire BA12 7NN
tel. (0985) 3551

Warrington:
Museum and Art Gallery, Bold Street, Warrington, Cheshire WA1 1JG
tel. (0925) 30550

Walton Hall, Walton Lea Road, Higher Walton, Warrington, Cheshire WA4 6SN
tel. (0925) 601617

Wednesbury:
Sandwell Art Gallery and Museum, Holyhead Road, Wednesbury, West Midlands WS1D 7DF
tel. (021) 556 0683

Welshpool:
Powis Castle, Powis Castle Park, Welshpool, Powys SY21 7DX
tel. (0938) 3001

Westcliff-on-Sea:
Beecroft Art Gallery, Station Road, Westcliff-on-Sea, Essex SS0 7RA
tel. (0702) 347418

Westerham:
Chartwell, Westerham, Kent TN16 1PS
tel. (073) 278 368

Wetherby:
Bramham Park, Wetherby, West Yorkshire LS23 6ND
tel. (0937) 844265

Whitby:
Pannett Art Gallery, Pannett Park, Whitby, North Yorkshire
tel. (0947) 602908

Whitehaven:
Whitehaven Museum and Art Gallery, Civic Hall, Lowther Street, Whitehaven, Cumbria CA28 7SH
tel. (0946) 3111, ext. 307

Winchester:
Guildhall Picture Gallery, The Guildhall, The Broadway, Winchester, Hampshire SO23 9ES
tel. (0962) 68166, ext. 289

Winchester City Museum, The Square, Winchester, Hampshire SO23 9ES
tel. (0962) 68166, ext. 269

The Winchester Gallery, School of Art, Park Avenue, Winchester, Hampshire SO23 8DL
tel. (0962) 61891

Windsor:
Brewhouse Gallery, Eton College, Windsor, Berkshire SL4 6DW
tel. (07535) 69991 (*opening times restricted*)

Guildhall, High Street, Windsor, Berkshire SL4 1LR
tel. (07535) 66167

The Royal Library, Windsor Castle, Windsor
tel. (07535) 68286

Woburn:
Woburn Abbey, Woburn, Bedfordshire MK43
0TP
tel. (0525) 26 666

Wolverhampton:
Bilston Museum and Art Gallery, Mount
Pleasant, Wolverhampton, West Midlands
WV14 7LS
tel. (0902) 409143

Central Art Gallery, Lichfield Street,
Wolverhampton, West Midlands WV1 1DU
tel. (0902) 312032

Wightwick Manor, Wolverhampton, West
Midlands WV6 8EE
tel. (0902) 761108

Worcester:
City Museum and Art Gallery, Foregate Street,
Worcester WR1 1DT
tel. (0905) 25371

Worthing:
Worthing Museum and Art Gallery, Chapel
Road, Worthing, West Sussex BN11 1HQ
tel. (0903) 39999, ext. 121

Wrexham:
Wrexham Library Arts Centre, Rhosddu Road,
Wrexham, Clwyd
tel. (0978) 261932

York:
Beningbrough Hall, nr York, North Yorkshire
tel. (0904) 470715

City of York Art Gallery, Exhibition Square,
York, North Yorkshire YO1 2EW
tel. (0904) 623839

Index

(See also Appendices)